C000184700

SAVOUR

SAVOUR

Salads for all Seasons

PETER GORDON

PHOTOGRAPHY BY LISA LINDER

To Al (and my London Fields)

First published in 2016 by
Jacqui Small LLP
74–77 White Lion Street London N1 9PF
Text copyright © 2016 by Peter Gordon
Design, photography and layout copyright
© Jacqui Small 2016

Publisher: Jacqui Small
Senior Commissioning Editor: Fritha Saunders
Managing Editor: Emma Heyworth-Dunn
Editor: Anne McDowall
Cover design, illustrations, text design and art
direction: Here Design
Production: Maeve Healy

ISBN: 9781910254493

A catalogue record for this book is available
from the British Library.

2018 2017 2016
10 9 8 7 6 5 4 3 2 1
Printed in China

Quarto is the authority on a wide range
of topics. Quarto educates, entertains
and enriches the lives of our readers —
enthusiasts and lovers of hands-on living.
www.QuartoKnows.com

Contents

Introduction

Salads have never been as varied or as exciting as they are right now! Today, the idea of having a salad as a main meal instead of just as a starter or side dish, no matter what the season, no longer seems as strange as it did a decade ago. We've come to appreciate that salads are not just for summer, they can be enjoyed all year round. From what I witness in my restaurants around the world, people are eating differently: sharing plates and small dishes are now commonplace, and the abundance of vegetables in a dish is almost a given. Healthy foods, whether that means more grains and vegetables, less gluten and dairy, less animal protein, sustainably caught fish or animals raised with impeccable farming methods, are what we all seem to want in our diets. These are all things I've been advocating, and the way I've been cooking and eating, for as long as I can remember – and salads are a terrific way to bring all of this together! In 2005, I wrote a much-loved book called Salads, the new main course. *This book is a way for me to update what I wrote a decade ago.*

I wanted to write a new book about salads that would inspire you to have the confidence to create an exciting meal just by looking at the ingredients you may already have in the pantry or your fridge. Admittedly, some recipes call for more preparation and shopping than others (though prepping artichoke hearts, podding broad/fava beans or poaching a chicken in a master-stock are all well worth the effort), but in the time-poor days that many of us lead, you can, of course, use prepared alternatives from the shop or freezer.

I love nothing more than combining a variety of flavours, textures and ingredients to make a new tasty salad. In summer, it may be a surprisingly delicious combination of heirloom tomatoes, burrata and a mango dressing; in autumn (the fall), a combo of beetroot (beet)-cured wild salmon with the last of the artichokes and pomegranate; while in winter it could be a warm salad of chicken livers, hazelnuts and mushrooms. What I like about salads is that they can suit your mood: they can be quick and easy (see Simple Salads, pages 22–43) or planned in advance and given the kind of focus a hot meal might receive. Some of the salads in this book are to be served at room temperature and others warm, but many can be served either way, so they needn't be seen as exclusively either winter or summer salads.

The elements of a salad

What defines a salad? Is it merely a few ingredients tossed together in a bowl with a dressing, or is it more complex than that? My view is that a salad is a mixture of ingredients, individually prepared (as opposed to cooked together in a stew), that work in harmony with each other, either by being very similar in texture and colour or by opposing each other, for example crunch supporting smooth. Some salads are elegantly plated assemblages while others are casually tossed together.

To create harmony, you sometimes need to create a clash of some sort. Adding a contrasting flavour or texture to a mix can often highlight other ingredients in the same dish. In these recipes, you'll discover, for example, the shock of a sweet roast grape that highlights sharp citrus notes, or fiery chilli used to enliven sweet mango.

Choosing your ingredients

Because salads are combinations of ingredients, it's very important that the produce you use is of premium quality – perhaps more so in salads than in cooked dishes as the ingredients often have very little done to them. If one of the ingredients isn't perfect, it can instantly ruin the dish.

Salad leaves should be plump and firm – no wilted leaves please (although a quick dip in cold water, a shake or a turn in a salad spinner to dry them, then 30 minutes in a plastic bag in the fridge can work wonders with greens and herbs).

Choose fruit and vegetables that are fresh, in season, ripe and unblemished. If you use a tomato in the middle of winter, then don't expect it to taste anything like the ones you had on vacation in the summer.

Fish should be sustainably caught and not under threat from over-fishing (this will really depend on where in the world you live). If they're farmed, then make sure they are from certified farms.

With poultry and meat, you should buy the best you can afford. Hopefully, this will mean that your meat has been produced with caring animal husbandry. Veal should be rose veal: avoid cage-reared white veal, which is a dreadful way of rearing these young male cattle. Chicken and eggs should ideally be organic, or at least properly free range (note that different countries have baffling versions of what free range actually means) and definitely not cage reared.

A note on quantities

I have taken a relaxed approach to quantities. When deciding how much rocket (arugula) it would require to feed four people, I decided that one or two handfuls were far easier and more realistic a quantity than 100 grams (3½oz.) or two bunches (how big a bunch is will depend on where you bought it). Ultimately, it's up to you to decide how much you want to serve; a little more or less will not ruin a dish.

Salt and spice

I have rather a large assortment of salt in my kitchen – Danish, British and New Zealand sea salt, smoked salt from numerous countries, pink Murray River salt from Australia and sulphurous black salt from India – and I like to play with the variety in my cooking. For boiling vegetables, I use inexpensive fine salt. But for all recipes in the book, unless specified otherwise, I have used flaky sea salt. It's worth noting that miso paste, soy sauce and fish sauce are also good salty seasoning agents; however, they will darken a salad dressing (and therefore the salad itself) as they tend to be brown. They will also add their own individual flavour, which can be good – or not – depending on the dish.

Chillies, while not a commonplace seasoning (unless you cook like me), are great used with all manner of foods. As a general rule, a small wrinkly chilli will be much hotter than a medium-sized smooth one. It is the fibres that hold the seeds to the body of the chilli that give the heat. If you aren't sure how hot your chilli is, then it's best to remove the green stem, cut the chilli in half lengthways and scrape the seeds and fibres out using a small teaspoon (run the spoon lengthways down the chilli). Add the body, usually chopped up, to the dish and taste it. If it could do with more heat, add a little of the chopped seeds and fibre – go gently and you'll be fine. It pays to wear gloves when preparing chillies as they have a habit of spicing up your fingers. Unless I have specified otherwise, don't remove the seeds. I have assumed the chillies you use will be medium heat in strength – use more or less to taste.

Extracting coconut from the shell

Coconut is one of my favourite flavours, as either creamy coconut milk or freshly grated (shredded) or toasted flesh. You can buy desiccated (shredded) coconut from shops, but if you are in a more adventurous mood, I suggest you attempt to prepare your own grated fresh coconut – it's infinitely better! The hard part is getting the flesh from the shell but it's not impossible. Select a coconut that feels heavy – if it's light then chances are the flesh may have deteriorated and dried out. In most countries apart from Asia, you'll be buying a coconut with a hard brown shell – either hairy or, if trimmed, smooth. Hold the coconut firmly in one hand, or rest it on a towel on the work-top, and hit it firmly with a pestle, a hammer, or the back of a meat cleaver in the centre (think of the centre as you would the equator on a globe), rotating it a few degrees after every hit. Eventually, after it's been rotated completely once or twice, you should hear it pop open. This will cause the liquid inside to drizzle or gush out – depending on how hard you've been hitting it. You can strain this liquid and drink it as long as it smells good. (Occasionally, I have opened a coconut only to discover the flesh has begun to rot a little – it smells very soapy – and have had to throw it away, which is very frustrating after all that effort.) The flesh should be white and firm with no trace of rot or discoloration. Once the coconut has popped, you'll need to prise the two sides apart – a large blunt knife, screwdriver or oyster knife is good for this. To make it easier to remove the white flesh from the brown shell, you can place the two halves on a baking sheet in an oven set to 170°C (350°F/Gas mark 4) and bake until the flesh begins to shrink back from the shell a little, about 15 minutes. Using either the knife, screwdriver or oyster knife, you need to prise the flesh away fully from the shell. It may come away in one piece but usually it'll break apart as you do so. Be careful though: it can be hard work and you don't want your knife to slip and cut you. Once you have the flesh out, you can then grate it or peel it into strips using a potato peeler, then eat it as it is or toast it on a baking sheet at 160°C (325°F/Gas mark 3) until golden. Turn it frequently to ensure that it cooks evenly.

Growing micro-greens and sprouts from seed

Throughout this book I sometimes use sprouts and cress. When I was doing my chef's apprenticeship I used to sprout mung beans, fenugreek seeds and mustard cress at home. However, these days the variety available through farmers' markets, supermarkets, food halls and better vegetable suppliers is extraordinary. When sprouting any seeds or grains the worst thing you can do is let them get waterlogged – they will rot. Make sure you keep them moist but not drowning in water.

Head to your local health food store: chances are they will have special jars for sprouting the likes of mung beans and chickpeas. These tend to be jars with a mesh lid that is screwed on. Put the seeds in the jar and soak overnight. The next day, drain the water from the jar and then begin a daily routine of wetting the grains and draining them. Eventually they'll sprout and you'll be able to eat this nutritious food source. These sprouting jars will have their own instructions.

Mustard cress is grown differently, and you can also use this method for growing the herb cresses (basil, coriander/cilantro, shiso, fenugreek, parsley). Line a shallow dish with cotton wool or thick tissues and dampen with water. Sprinkle generously with seeds (too few and they find it hard to grow straight) and leave in a light place (but avoid direct sunlight). Next day, moisten the cotton wool again. Leave for up to 3 weeks, ensuring that the cotton wool is kept damp but not waterlogged, or the sprouts will rot. Once the seeds sprout, they will shoot up quickly, but they should be at least 5cm (2in.) tall before you snip them at the base.

A micro-green is really just a fancy word for a baby salad leaf. The name seems to have originated in America and I can still remember seeing my first examples of them when I went for a job interview at Sign of the Dove restaurant in New York in 1987. The salad chef had the most tiny frisée (curly endive), rocket (arugula), red oak leaf and sorrel imaginable. He also had baby beetroot (beet) leaves and baby chard. I was amazed that they could be so small until I realized that they were simply the first stages of the plant's growth. These days, anyone with a garden or even a window box can grow them. Sow your seeds a little denser than normal and when they have grown to about 5–8cm (2–3in.), cut them 1cm (½in.) from the base. Store in an airtight bag in the fridge and use as soon as possible.

Adding crunch

A salad benefits from combining several different textures, from the crunchy texture derived from the addition of nuts or croutons to the soft one from goats' curd or a puréed vegetable. Much as a green salad with a little olive oil and lemon juice makes a great side dish, it won't leave your dinner guests satisfied if you serve it as a starter, but add a few roast grapes, toasted sunflower seeds and some shaved Parmesan and then you're talking! Focusing on texture is perhaps a more Southeast Asian approach to creating food than classic European, but it certainly adds to the final memory of a dish. Here are some tips for adding interesting crunch and flavours to your salads.

Toasting nuts
Nuts are perhaps the most commonly used crunchy ingredient. The rule of thumb when toasting them is to toast different types separately as they cook at different speeds. For example, a pine nut will cook in a quarter of the time that a Brazil nut will take, due to the difference in their size. I prefer to toast nuts in the oven rather than in a pan. Set your oven to 160°C (325°F/Gas mark 3), no higher or you risk burning them. Lay the nuts on a tray (in a single layer – don't try to toast them in bulk in a small roasting dish) and bake until they turn golden brown. Shake them from time to time to colour evenly. A pine nut will take about 8–10 minutes, a cashew about 15. You can also cook nuts in a dry pan, but I find this less effective and often the nut will burn in patches yet still be raw on the inside. If your nuts have skin on them – this is often how you buy hazelnuts, in particular – then toast them as described above and, once they have coloured, tip them into a tea (dish) towel and wrap them up. The steam that generates in the towel loosens the skin. Once they've cooled down to a temperature you are comfortable with, simply rub them together for a minute or so, still in the tea (dish) towel, and the skin will easily come off. To remove the skin from almonds, pour boiling water over them. Once they've cooled, the skin should come off fairly easily; if not, soak them again.

Caramelized boiled nuts
This method produces delicious shiny sweet crunchy cashews and peanuts. Place two handfuls of skinless nuts in a pan with a litre (4¼ cups) of cold water and a teaspoon of salt and bring to the boil. Cook cashews for 8 minutes and peanuts for 12 minutes. Drain into a colander, then tip into a bowl, add 4 tablespoons of

sugar and toss together. Tip onto a baking sheet lined with non-stick baking parchment and leave to cool and dry completely — you want the sugar to form a coating on the nuts and it's important that they are dry when you fry them. This may take overnight in a breezy or warm place. If you're in a hurry, you can also dry them in an oven set to 100°C (200°F/Gas mark ¼). Once they've dried out, separate any that have stuck together. Heat up a wok or frying pan (skillet) with 3cm (1¼in.) of peanut (groundnut) or sunflower oil to 160°C (325°F) and add one third of the nuts. Fry them, stirring constantly, until they turn a medium caramel colour. Don't overcook them as they will continue to cook for a few minutes even when you take them out of the oil. Remove with a slotted spoon and place on non-stick baking parchment or a baking sheet and leave to cool. (Don't do as I did once and lay them on absorbent kitchen paper — the caramel coating will stick to it and it's impossible to remove!) Leave to cool and store in an airtight jar.

Toasting larger seeds

Toasted pumpkin and sunflower seeds are the perfect way to add crunch for people with a nut allergy, plus they are generally less expensive than nuts. You can toast them on a baking sheet in the oven as you would nuts, but you can also sauté them in oil in a pan. The benefit of this method when cooking pumpkin seeds is that you end up with a lovely dark green oil, which tastes great and can be used in the finished salad as part of the dressing. Pour 3 tablespoons of oil into a smallish pan over a medium heat and add a generous handful of seeds. Slowly heat it up, stirring from time to time, and once the seeds begin sizzling, turn the heat down and cook until they turn a shade of golden. Immediately tip into a wide heatproof dish and leave to cool.

Soy sunflower seeds

These have their roots in macrobiotic cooking. Heat up a heavy-based frying pan (skillet) and add two handfuls of sunflower seeds. Toast in the pan over a medium–low heat, shaking and stirring frequently until they colour. Add 2 tablespoons of soy sauce or tamari (wheat-free soy sauce) and cook to evaporate it — stirring constantly. Once it has evaporated, tip them onto a plate and leave to cool. Separate any seeds that have joined together and store in an airtight jar.

Sesame seeds

Toasted sesame seeds add a really lovely savoury taste to a salad, as well as a little mouth-popping texture. However, toasting them can be a little messy as they pop all over the stove. In Japan, they have a special ceramic 'pot' that they toast seeds in. It has a lid and a spout — rather like an eccentric teapot. Assuming that you don't have such an implement, you can toast them either in the oven at 160°C (325°F/Gas mark 3) until golden or in small quantities in a saucepan with a lid. Shake them over a medium heat and when most have turned golden brown, tip them out to cool. You can also buy fabulous pre-toasted sesame seeds from Japanese and Korean food stores.

Popcorn

You might think that popcorn in salads is odd, but I was adding it to salads at The Sugar Club Restaurant in New Zealand as early as 1988 and it's delicious! Place a deep saucepan over a high heat, add enough peanut (groundnut) oil, refined olive oil or sunflower oil to give you about 3mm (⅛in.) depth, then quickly add 3 tablespoons of popcorn kernels (make sure you buy the correct corn). Cover the pan with a tight-fitting lid, then shake the pan gently, keeping it on the heat, until you hear the corn begin to pop. Continue to shake it gently, still on the heat, until the popping stops. Tip the corn into a bowl and leave to cool. Store in an airtight container.

Croutons

Croutons are a great salad addition: as well as providing a delicious crunch, they're also a good way to use up leftover bread. Simply slice or dice leftover stale bread (it'll be easier to slice if more than 2 days old) and toss or brush with enough oil to lightly coat. For sliced croutons, it's easier to lay them on a baking sheet and then either drizzle or brush the oil over them. Don't pile them on top of each other or they won't cook evenly. Bake in the oven at 160°C (325°F/Gas mark 3) and cook until golden. Alternatively, you can fry small diced croutons but they will absorb more oil. One of the nicest breads to make croutons from is Irish soda bread: the flavour and texture is lovely. Heavy, brown seed breads can sometimes produce very hard, teeth-shattering croutons. If that's the only bread you have, slice it wafer thin rather than into cubes.

Crispy shallots and garlic

These two ingredients are typical in Southeast Asian cuisine. They work well in salads that have garlic in the dressing or those with an abundance of fresh herbs. The best shallots to use are the small red ones from Thailand, although they can be hard to peel. Peel and thinly slice them, then toss with a little fine salt to absorb some of the moisture and leave for 30 minutes. Gently squeeze excess moisture from them, rinse briefly under cold water and shake in a sieve, then pat dry on absorbent kitchen paper. If you are using garlic, simply peel and thinly slice it (a mandolin is good for this). Place the sliced garlic or shallots into a wok or a pan and cover with 2.5–4cm (1–1½in.) of sunflower oil. Turn the heat to medium and gently stir to prevent the slices sticking together. Once they begin to sizzle, keep an eye on them, and as soon as they've gone to just beyond golden, remove with a slotted spoon or drain through a fine heatproof sieve and lay on absorbent kitchen paper. Once cooled, store in airtight containers. You can also buy these in Asian supermarkets, while in Indian shops, you'll find crispy onions, cooked the same way, which are great sprinkled over meat-based salads as well as curries.

Dressings

A dressing can make or ruin a salad. A simple dressing (oil and vinegar) helps moisten the salad, but a more complicated one can be the highlight. A dressing has to be in balance; that means the acidity and the oiliness need to work in harmony. However, you also need to think of the components in the dish — if you're using chunks of citrus fruit or grapes roasted with verjus or tamarind, then the dressing should not be too acidic or it'll make the whole dish way too sharp on the tongue. Likewise, if you're making a dressing to go with artichokes that are braised in olive oil, then make sure it isn't too oily or you will drown the dish in oil. When making a dressing, you can either whisk everything together in a small bowl or, which is even easier, simply put the ingredients in a jar, screw the lid on tight, then shake it all together.

Acidity to oil ratio

As a rule of thumb, I use three and a half or four parts of oil to one part of vinegar. To make enough dressing for four large green salads, use 2 tablespoons of oil to just under 1½ teaspoons of vinegar. However, if I'm using lemon juice, pomegranate molasses or verjus instead of vinegar, then I use a slightly higher ratio of the acidic component (about three to one) as all three are less acidic than vinegar.

Acidity and sourness

The range of vinegars available these days is incredible. In my local shops in Hackney in London, they have so many different types, from coconut vinegar to sherry vinegar, as well as red wine vinegar from numerous countries, apple and cider vinegar, rice vinegar and various types of balsamic vinegar. All these types of vinegar have hugely differing characteristics.

You can also get acidity and sourness from other ingredients, my favourites being pomegranate molasses, verjus (made from unfermented grapes, this needs to be kept in the fridge once opened or it will go off), tamarind (you can extract the sourness yourself by soaking and squashing the pulp of the fruit in warm water, then passing it through a sieve — or buy a generally less potent pre-made paste) and the juice of citrus fruit — from lemons through to grapefruit, oranges, yuzu and limes. Remember, too, that it's not just the juice from citrus fruit that will give flavour to a salad — the finely grated zest, the colourful outer layer of the skin, will also add character. Buy unwaxed fruit in preference to waxed if available. However, the modern world being what it is, the chances are that the fruit you buy will have had a fine layer of wax sprayed onto it to help preserve it and you'll need to rub this off with a warm cloth or paper towel before grating the zest.

Oils

As with vinegar, there is a huge variety of oils to choose from. The less flavoursome ones — and therefore those to use when you want the 'salad ingredients' to stand out as the heroes of the dish — include sunflower, grape seed, light olive oil and what is often termed 'vegetable salad oil'.

Nut oils, most commonly walnut, hazelnut, almond and peanut (groundnut) oil add flavour, although almond and peanut (groundnut) oils are very subtle. There are also toasted nut oils on the market, which have a more pronounced flavour. These can sometimes be a little overbearing in a dressing, however, so you may want to dilute them with some plain oil. Toasted sesame oil has a wonderful flavour but you do need to use it sparingly. Argan oil is less commonly known but is a delicious oil well worth looking for. It's expensive, which won't help it become popular any time soon, but the process by which it is produced in Morocco is incredibly time consuming. If you see it and feel like splashing out, then do try it in a simple salad dressing for green leaves — I guarantee you'll be intrigued by its sweet nutty flavour.

Olive oils could provide the subject for a book in themselves, but basically, an extra virgin olive oil has much lower acidity than virgin or 'plain' olive oil. An extra virgin olive oil begins to lose its grassy fresh flavours after 12–18 months, so try to buy a new season's oil that has been dated so you aren't disappointed when you drizzle it over your salad.

Avocado oil is produced by crushing avocado flesh and extracting the oil from it in the same way that oil is extracted from olives. It's also great to cook with as it has a high smoke point (which means the flavour doesn't taste burnt or deteriorate as it gets hot), so it's perfect for frying fish fillets or chicken breasts (fillets), barbecuing and roasting.

You can now also buy oils flavoured with chilli, lemon, truffle, herbs, garlic and numerous other flavours, but do bear in mind that they won't all taste great. With all oils, it's important to keep them in a cool place, away from any heat and sunlight, and to use them up fairly quickly once opened.

Simple Salads

CHAPTER 1

Red salad

AT ROOM TEMPERATURE

INGREDIENTS

2 red (bell) peppers

1 radicchio

3 plum tomatoes

1 beetroot (beet)

4 tbsp pomegranate seeds

2 tbsp sesame seeds, toasted

½ medium-heat chilli, finely chopped, including the seeds

2 tbsp red wine vinegar

1 tsp caster (superfine) sugar

3 tbsp extra virgin olive oil

1 tsp flaky salt

This is a chunky version of a favourite salad of mine, 'salsa rossa', which I use to dress grilled (broiled) fish and meats. This salad is also lovely mixed into a simple risotto with lots of Parmesan.

[METHOD]

Grill (broil) and peel the peppers (see page 34) and cut them into strips.

Discard the outer leaves of the radicchio if bruised, cut into quarters lengthways, discard the white stem, then thinly shred.

Cut the tomatoes into large dice.

Peel and thinly slice the beetroot (I used a striped beet and sliced it using a mandolin).

Put all the ingredients into a bowl and toss together thoroughly. Leave for 10 minutes, then taste for seasoning and serve.

FOR 6–8 AS A SIDE DISH

White-ish salad

AT ROOM TEMPERATURE

INGREDIENTS

1 long cucumber

1 head fennel, any blemished parts removed

1 small celeriac

1 kohlrabi

Rather like coleslaw, this salad is great tucked into a bun with a barbecued beef patty or a piece of grilled (broiled) salmon. It's also good served with a roast chicken or smoked ham. For the dressing, use either the egg-free milk aioli or the mayonnaise from the dressings chapter (see pages 266 and 264 respectively) or plain yogurt or crème fraîche (thick sour cream) – whatever you have to hand. Use a mandolin to slice everything as thinly as possible.

200g (7oz./2 cups) green grapes, sliced or halved, depending on their size

200g (7oz.) yellow beans, blanched, refreshed and cut into 2.5cm (1in.) lengths (about 1 cup prepped)

2 tbsp lemon juice

1 tsp flaky salt

100g (3½oz./½ cup) milk aioli or mayonnaise (see pages 266 and 264) or crème fraîche (thick sour cream) or yogurt (see recipe introduction)

[METHOD]

Peel the cucumber, cut it in half lengthways and remove the seeds, then slice it crossways into thin half-circles.

Thinly slice the fennel crossways into rings, discarding the lower 1cm (½in.), which can be a little fibrous.

Peel the celeriac and cut it into juliennes.

Peel the kohlrabi, cut it in half, then thinly slice it.

Toss everything together gently but thoroughly. Leave for 10 minutes, then taste for seasoning and serve.

FOR 6–8 AS A SIDE DISH

Green salad

AT ROOM TEMPERATURE

INGREDIENTS

350g (12oz.) edamame beans in their pods

50g (1¾ oz./⅓ cup) peas, fresh or frozen

300g (10½oz.) asparagus

2 courgettes (zucchini)

1 long cucumber

1 generous handful flat-leaf (Italian) parsley leaves, shredded

20 mint leaves, shredded

20 basil leaves, shredded

100g (3½oz./1½ cups) pea shoots (or use wild rocket/arugula or frisée/curly endive)

3 tbsp extra virgin olive oil

1 tbsp lemon juice

½ tsp flaky salt

This is so simple it almost doesn't need a recipe, but it's really here as a reminder of what you could use when in season. A summer-raised courgette (zucchini) will be infinitely better than one from a hothouse in winter, so use what's best at the time. Different shades of green from the different ingredients – and the more the merrier – will make it look really good. A mandolin is good to use for all this slicing.

[METHOD]

Boil the edamame in their pods (if they've been frozen from raw, they'll need 4 minutes; if pre-cooked then frozen, only 30 seconds). Drain, refresh in iced water and remove the beans from their pods.

Boil the peas for 1 minute, then refresh them in iced water and drain.

Snap off the hard ends of the asparagus stalks and discard, then slice on an angle.

Top and tail the courgettes (zucchini) and cucumber and thinly slice them.

Put all the ingredients into a bowl, toss together, then serve immediately.

FOR 4–6 AS A SIDE DISH

Kale and preserved lemon couscous

WARM OR AT ROOM TEMPERATURE

INGREDIENTS

150g (5½oz./scant 1 cup) instant couscous

250g (9oz.) kale, woody stems removed

20 mint leaves

2 tbsp extra virgin olive oil

1 small preserved lemon (80g/3oz.)

This green couscous is a really good way to have a grain and a vegetable at the same time, and friends with children have told me it's a handy recipe to have up their sleeves when they're trying to get the family to eat veggies. I've made this many times using blanched broccoli instead of kale, and you can also use blanched or raw cauliflower or carrots and any herb that takes your fancy. Always use tepid or cold rather than boiling water when making couscous to prevent it going soggy. It can be successfully microwaved to heat it up if necessary.

[METHOD]

In a medium bowl, mix the couscous with 220ml (scant 1 cup) tepid water and ¾ teaspoon of salt. Leave until the water has been absorbed.

Boil or steam the kale for 3 minutes. Drain into a colander, run cold water over for 20 seconds, then refresh in iced water. Drain again and squeeze out excess water.

Put the kale in a food processor with the mint leaves and olive oil and blitz in several short bursts, scraping down the side of the bowl each time, until you have coarse crumbs. (Don't purée it smooth.)

Cut the lemon in half and scoop out the flesh with a teaspoon then squeeze it through a sieve into a small bowl. Discard any pips and flesh. Finely chop the lemon rind and mix with the juice.

Mix the blitzed kale and the lemon into the couscous with a generous amount of freshly ground black pepper, adding salt to taste.

For a picture of the finished dish, see page 32, top.

FOR 4 AS A SIDE DISH

Watermelon and feta with sumac and capers

AT ROOM TEMPERATURE

INGREDIENTS

600g (1lb. 5oz.) watermelon flesh, cut into chunks

150g (5½oz.) feta, roughly crumbled (1 cup crumbled)

2 tsp baby capers, rinsed and patted dry

20 mint leaves, torn

1 tbsp sumac

2 tbsp lemon juice

1 tbsp extra virgin olive oil

I wrote a recipe for a feta and watermelon salad in my first cookbook, The Sugar Club Cookbook, way back in 1996. So, while it's not an original – and I'm pretty sure the salad originated in Israel – here's a little twist on my first attempt. Sumac, an astringent red powder made from ground dried berries from the Middle East, works a treat with the sweetness of the watermelon. Mint adds a refreshing top note to the salad and the salty capers add bite and seasoning.

[METHOD]

Mix everything together and serve immediately.

FOR 8 AS A SIDE DISH

Minted baby potatoes, peas and crème fraîche

WARM OR AT ROOM TEMPERATURE

INGREDIENTS

750g (1lb. 10oz.) baby potatoes, skins scrubbed if dirty

250g (9oz./1⅔ cups) peas, fresh or frozen (if using fresh in the pod, you'll need just over 500g/1lb. 2oz.)

8 shallots, or 2 banana shallots, thinly sliced

1 tbsp vegetable oil

200g (7oz./generous ¾ cup) crème fraîche (thick sour cream)

40 mint leaves (1 loose handful), shredded

If you're lucky enough to be able to source Jersey Royal potatoes, then these are ideal here; otherwise, use a good, small potato as I have done. When I was growing up in Whanganui, New Zealand, we would head off once a year with Dad and Rose and dig up what we called 'pig potatoes', which I think were named after the creatures that would eat the potatoes that hadn't been harvested by machine – if we didn't get to them first! Serve this warm or at room temperature.

[METHOD]

Boil the potatoes in lightly salted water until almost done (when you can insert a knife through them). Add the peas and cook for an additional 2 minutes. Drain into a colander and run cold water over them for a few minutes, then drain again.

While the potatoes are cooking, sauté the shallots in the oil with ¼ teaspoon of salt over a medium heat, stirring frequently, until caramelized and slightly crisp. Tip into a bowl and stir in the crème fraîche (thick sour cream).

Tip the potatoes and peas into a large bowl and add the shallots and the mint. Stir together and taste for seasoning. Transfer into a clean bowl.

FOR 4 AS A SIDE DISH

Tomato, bread, sumac and basil

AT ROOM TEMPERATURE

INGREDIENTS

3 slices sourdough bread (about 130g/4½oz.), a few days old

3 tbsp olive oil

250g (9oz.) cherry tomatoes, quartered

1 tbsp sumac

3 tbsp red wine vinegar

20 basil leaves, roughly torn

20 mint leaves, roughly torn

1 tsp young marjoram or oregano leaves

There are many versions of this salad to be found around the Mediterranean, from Italy's panzanella through to Tunisia's fatoush. Mine is very simple and is best served as one of several salads on a table. You can make it much more substantial by adding lots of peeled diced cucumber, grilled (broiled) peppers, radishes and lettuce. The bread needs to be a few days old – like breadcrumbs, which were always made at home when I was a child, it's a good way to use up stale bread instead of throwing it out. Use a variety of coloured cherry tomatoes if you have them to hand – they'll look great.

[METHOD]

Cut the bread into cubes and soak in cold water for 10 minutes. Drain, then squeeze out excess moisture and place in a bowl.

Add everything else along with ½ teaspoon of salt and ¼ teaspoon of freshly ground black pepper. Toss together well and leave for 10 minutes. Toss again and taste for seasoning.

Grilled peppers with dill

AT ROOM TEMPERATURE

INGREDIENTS

6 (bell) peppers

3 tbsp olive oil

½ tsp lemon zest

juice of 1 lemon

3 tbsp snipped dill

Use fleshy sweet red or yellow (bell) peppers at the height of summer for this recipe rather than green ones, which in my opinion are good only for eating raw. You can use canned peppers, but they always have a slightly metallic taste to them and will be less successful. There are as many ways to cook and peel a pepper as there are months in the year, but for those of you with gas burners on your stove, this first method is my preferred technique – just make sure you have the extraction on and any doors shut that could cause your fire detector to be set off. If you don't have gas burners, then do them the second way. These peppers are lovely served as part of a mezze – just as they would be in Turkey and Greece.

[METHOD]

To peel the pepper, if you have a stove with gas burners: turn them on and sit the peppers on the flame, or rest them against it, rotating them as they blacken. Don't incinerate them completely, but make sure that they are blackened and blistered all over. As they're done, place them in a heatproof bowl and when all are done, cover tightly with cling film (plastic wrap) and leave to cool for 15 minutes. Once cooled, take them out, pull off the stalk and split each pepper in half lengthways. Peel off the skin and remove the seeds. (It can help to do this under very gently running cold water but it's not necessary.)

Alternatively, turn your oven grill (broiler) to high. Cut the peppers lengthways into quarters and remove the stalk and seeds. Brush the outer, shiny skin sides with a little of the oil and sit the quarters on a baking sheet, skin sides facing up. Place under the grill (broiler) and cook for 8–10 minutes, or until the skins have blistered and blackened. When they're done, place in a heatproof bowl, cover tightly with cling film (plastic wrap) and leave to cool for 15 minutes. Peel off the skins.

Cut the peeled peppers lengthways into strips about 1cm (½in.) wide. Place in a bowl with the olive oil, lemon zest and juice and the dill. Add salt and pepper and mix it all together.

FOR 8 AS A SIDE DISH

Cabbage, apple, mint and sesame

AT ROOM TEMPERATURE

INGREDIENTS

500g (1lb. 2oz.) cabbage, thick stem removed and any blemished leaves discarded

90ml (6 tbsp/⅓ cup) cider or other white vinegar

3 apples (or use nashi pears or regular pears)

40 mint leaves

2 tbsp toasted sesame seeds

2 tbsp sesame oil

Use whatever cabbage you like, or a mix of several types (I used half Savoy cabbage and half firm white cabbage), but if you use red cabbage, be aware that the colour may seep into the other ingredients, so serve it as soon as you've made it. Choose an apple that suits your mood – some are sweeter than others – or replace with pears or nashi. A mandolin or the slicing blade in a food processor will help get the slices as thin as possible.

[METHOD]

Slice the cabbage as thin as you can, gently break it apart into strands and put into a bowl. (Red cabbage is quite dense and will want to stay connected whereas a Chinese cabbage will fall apart more easily.) Drizzle 4 tablespoons of the vinegar over it, add 2 teaspoons of salt and mix well, then cover and set aside for 30 minutes.

Tip the cabbage into a colander to drain away excess liquid, then transfer to a large bowl and mix in the remaining 2 tablespoons of vinegar.

Quarter the apples and remove the core, then thinly slice them and add to the bowl along with the mint, sesame seeds and sesame oil. Toss everything together and taste for seasoning.

FOR 6—8 AS A SIDE DISH

Beans, cashews, lemon and ginger

WARM OR AT ROOM TEMPERATURE

INGREDIENTS

1 small preserved lemon
(80g/3oz.)

3 tbsp lemon juice

2 tsp finely chopped ginger

1 tsp caster (superfine) sugar

3 tbsp extra virgin olive oil

600g (1lb. 5oz.) beans,
topped and tailed, blanched
and refreshed (I used a
mixture of yellow, runner/
pole and green beans and
mangetout/snow peas)

150g (5½oz./1 cup) cashews,
toasted and chopped

Make this when yellow beans are available. It couldn't be simpler, but I must stress that it works best when the beans are a little overcooked. Fine green beans are lovely with a crunch to them, but I find larger beans suit being more well done. If you don't have a preserved lemon, then peel the skin from a lemon and boil it for 4 minutes before chopping it, and add 2 teaspoons of extra lemon juice to the dressing.

[METHOD]

Cut the lemon in half and scoop out the flesh with a teaspoon then squeeze it through a sieve into a small bowl. Discard any pips and flesh. Finely chop the lemon rind and mix with the juice. Add the fresh lemon juice, ginger and sugar. Stir to dissolve the sugar. Whisk in the olive oil and taste for seasoning. The preserved lemon will be salty, so you won't need to add much at all.

Toss the beans, dressing and two thirds of the cashews together and place in a bowl. Scatter the remaining cashews on top.

Chickpeas, feta, spicy red onions, cumin and mint

WARM OR AT ROOM TEMPERATURE

_____

INGREDIENTS

75ml (5 tbsp) olive oil

2 red onions, thinly sliced

6 garlic cloves, thinly sliced

2 tsp chopped rosemary

1 red or green chilli, thinly sliced, including seeds

1 tsp cumin seeds

2 x 400g (14oz.) cans chickpeas, drained and rinsed (or use 500g/1lb. 2oz./3 cups cooked chickpeas)

3 tbsp lemon juice

8 strips lemon peel, julienned

200g (7oz.) feta, diced

1 handful flat-leaf (Italian) parsley leaves

1 handful mint leaves, torn if large

Using canned chickpeas is fine for this salad, unless of course you'd like to cook them from dried (see page 79). This is terrific served with grilled (broiled) squid or cuttlefish on top, but it also goes really well with roast lamb or chicken, baked on a pizza base, or served with a crispy fried egg or two for a weekend brunch. The quantity of oil here may seem excessive, but it's delicious when mopped up with bread.

[METHOD]

Sit a wide saucepan over a medium heat. Add 4 tablespoons of the oil, then sauté the onions, garlic, rosemary, chilli and cumin seeds until caramelized, stirring often as they cook.

Add the chickpeas, lemon juice and lemon peel and 1 teaspoon of salt, and simmer until most of the liquid has evaporated, stirring often. Tip into a bowl and leave to cool if serving at room temperature.

Add the feta, parsley, mint and remaining 1 tablespoon of olive oil and mix everything together. Taste for seasoning.

FOR 4–6 AS A SIDE DISH

Orange, pine nut and shallot

AT ROOM TEMPERATURE

INGREDIENTS

3 tbsp orange juice

2 shallots or 1 banana shallot, very thinly sliced into rings

2 oranges

2 tbsp pine nuts, toasted

2 tbsp extra virgin olive oil

12–15 small basil leaves (I used opal or purple basil)

I once had a salad similar to this near Seville in Spain and was amazed that unpeeled oranges could be so fabulous. (They also appealed to my lazy side!) Choose juicy oranges with firm skin, and make sure they're not too large or there will be too much bitter pith. Serve this salad alongside roast pork or duck, or with a soft cheese on top as a starter: burrata or slices of young pecorino or manchego work really well.

[METHOD]

Mix the orange juice with the shallots, separating the rings. Macerate for 20 minutes.

Cut the top and bottom 1cm (½in.) from each orange and discard. Slice them as thin as you can and lay on a plate. Remove any pips.

To serve, drain the juice from the shallots and lay over the orange slices. Scatter the pine nuts on top, drizzle with the olive oil, sprinkle with flaky salt, then scatter over the basil leaves.

Veggie Straight Up

_____

CHAPTER 2

Nashi, radish, ginger and cashews

AT ROOM TEMPERATURE

INGREDIENTS

1 small red onion, thinly sliced into rings

1 spring onion (scallion), thinly sliced

4 tbsp tahini

2 tbsp pomegranate molasses

1 tbsp finely chopped or grated ginger

2 tbsp sunflower oil

2 nashi pears (or use 3 apples)

3 celery stalks from the inside of the head, thinly sliced, plus any good-looking young leaves

1 handful baby radishes (or use 8 larger ones, quartered)

FOR THE CASHEWS

100g (3½oz./⅔ cup) cashews (untoasted)

½ tsp chilli flakes (optional)

1 tbsp sugar (any type will work)

1 tsp coriander seeds

This refreshing crunchy salad makes a great accompaniment to roast pork, chicken or duck, but equally it's a good component of a vegetarian spread. Nashi are a type of crunchy pear – also known as Asian pears – that are mildly sweet. If you can't find them, then use any crisp ripe apple or pear, or jicama. I like to cook cashews this way, and I also cook peanuts similarly, as the texture of the nuts changes quite noticeably. But if you're short of time, then just replace them with toasted cashews, to which you can add some toasted, pounded coriander seeds.

[METHOD]

First prepare the cashews. Put them in a medium saucepan with the chilli flakes, sugar, 400ml (1⅔ cups) of water and ¼ teaspoon of salt. Bring to the boil, then reduce the heat to a gentle boil and cook for 15 minutes. Don't let the liquid drop below the level of the nuts. If it does, top up with boiling water. Leave to cool in the pan, then drain in a colander and leave for 15 minutes. Tip into a baking dish lined with baking parchment and leave at room temperature overnight.

The next day, preheat the oven to 160°C (325°F/Gas mark 3) and bake the cashews until golden, about 45 minutes. Add the coriander seeds and cook until they're aromatic, about 5 minutes. Take from the oven and leave to cool. (Alternatively, you can deep-fry them, see pages 14—16.) Pound in a mortar and pestle to roughly smash them up. They can be kept in an airtight container for up to 2 weeks.

Place the red onion in a bowl and sprinkle with ½ teaspoon of fine salt. Firmly rub the salt into the onion, then leave at room temperature for 20 minutes. Rinse in a sieve under cold water and drain.

Rinse the spring onion (scallion) in a sieve under gently running cold water for a minute, then drain.

Stir the tahini with 100ml (scant ½ cup) of cold water until emulsified. Mix in the pomegranate molasses, ginger and sunflower oil. Season with salt to taste.

Cut the nashi into quarters, remove the core, then cut into fat batons, or slice 3mm (⅛in.) thick, and put in a bowl. Add the celery, celery leaves, red onion, spring onion (scallion), half the cashews and the dressing. Toss everything together, then sprinkle with the remaining cashews and the radishes.

47

Roast root veggies and pumpkin with creamy minted peas

WARM

INGREDIENTS

2 parsnips, peeled and cut into chunks

2 medium swedes (rutabaga), peeled and cut into chunks

2 carrots, peeled and cut into chunks

500g (1lb. 2oz.) pumpkin, peeled, deseeded and cut into chunks

60g (2¼oz./½ cup) pumpkin seeds

2 tsp coarsely chopped fresh sage

1 tsp fresh thyme leaves

3 large shallots (or use 2 smallish white-fleshed onions)

2 tbsp extra virgin olive oil

20g (¾oz./4 tsp) butter

200ml (¾ cup + 2 tsp) cream

250g (9oz./1⅔ cups) peas

20 mint leaves, shredded

20 basil leaves, shredded

1 small handful flat-leaf (Italian) parsley leaves, shredded

A lovely warm salad served in the middle of the table to accompany dinner, whether that be steamed chicken breast (fillet), grilled (broiled) venison chop, corned beef or roast cod. Frozen peas are what you'll be using in winter when most of the rest of the ingredients are in season, but come summer, use freshly podded ones with butternut squash and Jerusalem artichokes.

[METHOD]

Preheat the oven to 170°C (350°F/Gas mark 4).

Put the chunks of parsnip, swede (rutabaga), carrots and pumpkin in a roasting dish with the pumpkin seeds, sage and thyme. Thickly slice two of the shallots and add to the other vegetables along with 2 tablespoons of water, the oil, some salt and pepper, and toss it all together. Roast, tossing occasionally, until the vegetables are cooked, which will take about an hour.

When the vegetables are almost ready, dice the remaining shallot and sauté over a medium heat in the butter with a pinch of salt until golden. (Cover the pan to prevent the shallot burning and catching.) Add the cream and peas and bring to the boil, then cook on a rapid simmer for 2 minutes. Mix in half the mint just before serving and taste for seasoning.

To serve, transfer the roast veggies to a heatproof serving bowl, spoon the peas and their creamy sauce on top and scatter with the remaining mint and the basil and parsley.

FOR 8 AS A SIDE DISH

Chilli-roast sweet potato, courgettes, roast garlic, hazelnuts and pears

WARM OR AT ROOM TEMPERATURE

INGREDIENTS

1 head garlic, broken into separate (unpeeled) cloves

1kg (2lb. 4oz.) sweet potatoes, skins scrubbed, cut lengthways into wedges

2 large pears, halved, core removed, cut into thin wedges

1 or 2 red chillies, thinly sliced

1 tbsp rosemary leaves

2 tbsp olive oil

2 tbsp sesame oil

3 courgettes (zucchini) (600g/1lb. 5oz.), quartered lengthways

100g (3½oz./⅔ cup) hazelnuts, skins off, roughly chopped

100g (3½oz.) baby spinach (or use large-leaf spinach and coarsely shred it)

This is one for the middle of the table, although it would also make a tasty starter with large chunks of goats' curd dolloped on top, or even some thinly sliced smoked chicken breast (fillet). You don't need to boil the garlic in advance, but it makes it a little more mellow.

[METHOD]

Preheat the oven to 180°C (350°F/Gas mark 4).

Put the garlic in a pan, cover with 3cm (1¼in.) water and add ½ teaspoon of fine salt. Bring to the boil, then cook over a medium heat until the water has almost evaporated. Drain.

Put the garlic, sweet potatoes, pears, chillies, rosemary, olive oil and half the sesame oil into a roasting dish. Sprinkle on 1 teaspoon of salt and plenty of freshly ground black pepper. Roast in the oven for 45 minutes, tossing twice.

Add the courgettes (zucchini), hazelnuts and remaining sesame oil and toss together, then cook until the pears and sweet potato are cooked through, about 20 minutes.

Remove from the oven and stir in the spinach.

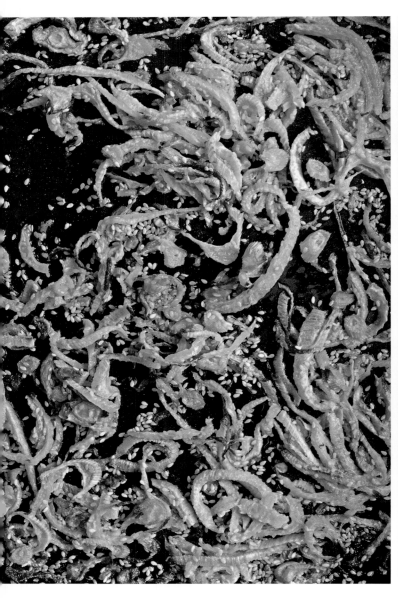

FOR 6 AS A STARTER OR 8–10 AS A SIDE DISH

Celeriac, satsuma, pear, fennel and red cabbage

AT ROOM TEMPERATURE

INGREDIENTS

2 tbsp sunflower oil

2 white-fleshed onions, thinly sliced

1 large celeriac (about 750g/ 1lb. 10oz.), peeled and cut into 3cm (1¼in.) chunks

3 pears, firm and ripe

2 satsumas (or use tangerines or clementines), unpeeled, halved, each half cut into 6–8 chunks and pips discarded

85ml (⅓ cup) lemon juice

4 tbsp extra virgin olive oil

2 heads fennel, trimmed and thinly sliced into rings

2 tbsp sesame seeds

¼ red cabbage (about 250g/9oz.), core discarded

I first enjoyed the combination of chilled cooked celeriac with tangerines and pear in Istanbul at Muzedechanga – a gorgeous terrace restaurant nestled on the Bosphorus that I've been a consultant to for many years, along with its sister restaurant Changa. It serves contemporary versions of traditional dishes, as well as fantastic new dishes created by its owners, Tarik and Savas. I've served the salad as part of a starter or main course with grilled (broiled) mackerel or some spiced lamb chops, but it's equally fabulous as a vegetarian starter, with cabbage and roast fennel mixed into it.

[METHOD]

Preheat the oven to 180°C (350°F/Gas mark 4).

Warm a medium pan over a medium heat. Add the sunflower oil and onions and 1½ teaspoons of flaky salt. Sauté with the lid on, without colouring, until wilted, stirring as it cooks.

Mix in the celeriac and cook, covered, on a slightly reduced heat, stirring every few minutes, for 10 minutes. Halve and core the pears, then cut each half into six chunks. Add these to the celeriac, along with the satsumas, lemon juice and 2 tablespoons of olive oil. Stir well, place a paper cartouche on top of the mixture, cover with a lid and cook for 15–20 minutes, stirring from time to time to prevent the vegetables catching on the base of the pan, until you can insert a knife through the celeriac with barely any resistance. Leave to cool in the pan, then taste for seasoning.

Meanwhile, toss the fennel with the remaining 2 tablespoons of olive oil, the sesame seeds and ½ teaspoon of salt. Roast in a baking dish until beginning to caramelize, about 20 minutes, stirring several times.

Slice the cabbage as thin as possible – a mandolin is good for this.

To serve, toss the cabbage with the fennel, taste for seasoning and lay it on your plates. Give the celeriac a gentle stir, taste for seasoning and spoon this and its juices on top.

Spiced roast cauliflower and garlic with tahini yogurt dressing

WARM OR AT ROOM TEMPERATURE

INGREDIENTS

1 large cauliflower, green leaves and excess stalk removed

1 red chilli, chopped

4 garlic cloves, sliced

3 tbsp sesame seeds

2 tbsp nigella seeds

4 green cardamom pods, crushed

1 tbsp olive oil

1 small handful parsley leaves

1 small handful mixed soft herbs (e.g. mint, basil, tarragon)

FOR THE TAHINI YOGURT DRESSING

2 tbsp tahini paste

1 tbsp lemon juice

100ml (scant ½ cup) Greek-style plain yogurt

½ tsp finely grated lemon zest

2 tbsp olive oil

This goes well with pretty much anything, from grilled (broiled) tuna steak or sausage to roast chicken or a slow-braised shoulder of lamb. Alternatively, for a vegetarian starter, scatter it with rocket (arugula) leaves, toasted nuts and pomegranate seeds or serve with chunks of roast butternut squash.

[METHOD]

Preheat the oven to 180°C (350°F/Gas mark 4).

Cut the cauliflower into florets and place in a roasting dish with the chilli, garlic, sesame seeds, nigella seeds, cardamom, the 1 tablespoon of olive oil and a little salt. Toss everything together and roast, tossing occasionally, until the cauliflower browns at the edges and the garlic become golden, about 30 minutes. If the garlic begins to darken before the cauliflower is ready, add 2 tablespoons of water to the roasting dish. Remove from the oven and leave to cool (unless you want to serve it warm).

Mix the tahini to a slurry with the lemon juice and 5 tablespoons of water. Stir in the yogurt, lemon zest and olive oil. Season with salt.

To serve, toss the cauliflower with the dressing and herbs.

Roast cauliflower, seeds, olives, green and broad beans and peas

WARM OR AT ROOM TEMPERATURE

INGREDIENTS

1 large cauliflower, green leaves and excess stalk removed

1 red (bell) pepper, seeds and stalk discarded, cut into pieces

2 tbsp sesame seeds

50g (1¾oz./scant ½ cup) pumpkin seeds

50g (1¾oz./⅓ cup) sunflower seeds

6 garlic cloves, sliced

2 tbsp olive oil

300g (10½oz./about 1⅔ cups) unpitted olives

150g (5½oz.) podded broad (fava) beans

200g (7oz.) green beans, topped and tailed if needed, cut into 4cm lengths (about 1⅓ cups prepped)

100g (3½oz./⅔ cup) peas, fresh or frozen and defrosted

This is a lovely dish served warm or at room temperature, and it's all the better if you can source different-coloured cauliflower: I used some romanesco broccoli, along with white and purple cauliflowers. For the seeds, use anything you have at hand – they add a lovely crunch to the salad. You can also use any type of olive, although avoid pitted ones as they generally aren't the best. If you are serving this warm, then don't refresh the beans, peas or broad (fava) beans: simply mix them into the cauliflower straight from the oven.

[METHOD]

Preheat the oven to 180°C (350°C/Gas mark 4).

Cut the cauliflower into florets and place into a large roasting dish with the pepper, seeds, garlic, olive oil and olives. Sprinkle over 1 heaped teaspoon of flaky salt and ¼ teaspoon of freshly ground black pepper. Roast until the white cauliflower has turned golden, about 30 minutes, tossing every 10 minutes. Remove from the oven and leave to cool.

Meanwhile, half-fill a medium pan with water, add 1 teaspoon of fine salt and bring to the boil.

Add the broad (fava) beans and boil for 2–3 minutes depending on their size. Remove the beans from the pan using a slotted spoon and refresh in iced water. Peel when cool enough to handle.

Add the green beans to the boiling water and cook for 2 minutes, then add the peas and boil for an additional 1 minute. Drain into a colander, refresh in iced water for a few minutes, then drain again.

To serve, toss the broad (fava) beans, green beans and peas with the cauliflower and season with salt to taste.

FOR 4 AS A STARTER

Asparagus, almonds, spiced quail eggs and shiitake with miso dressing

SLIGHTLY CHILLED OR AT ROOM TEMPERATURE

INGREDIENTS

1 tsp coriander seeds

½ tsp nigella seeds

¼ tsp cumin seeds

¼ tsp fennel seeds

12 quail eggs

1 tbsp white vinegar

300g (10½oz.) fresh shiitake mushrooms, stalks removed and discarded

800g (1lb. 12oz.) asparagus

1 handful salad leaves (I used pea shoots)

1 tbsp lemon juice

100g (3½oz./⅔ cup) almonds, toasted and roughly chopped (I used delicious marcona almonds from Spain)

FOR THE MISO DRESSING

1 tbsp soy sauce

2 tbsp mirin

1 tbsp miso paste (I used shiromiso)

2 tsp finely chopped or grated ginger

This is a really pretty, elegant salad full of popping tastes and contrasting textures. Quail eggs are tricky things to peel – use your fingernails and a small sharp knife – but well worth the effort. If you can't get them, then use hen's eggs and serve one per person.

[METHOD]

Lightly toast the coriander, nigella, cumin and fennel seeds in a dry frying pan (skillet) over a medium heat until they become aromatic. Leave to cool. Add ½ teaspoon of flaky salt and grind the spices in a spice grinder or using a mortar and pestle.

Place the quail eggs in a pan large enough to hold them in a single layer. Pour in enough water to cover by 3cm (1¼in.), add the vinegar, bring to the boil and cook for 3 minutes. Drain into a sieve or colander, then place in a bowl of iced water and leave for 5 minutes. Peel the eggs and roll them in the ground spices.

To make the dressing, mix the soy, mirin, miso paste and ginger until the miso has 'dissolved', then stir in 2 tablespoons of warm water.

Bring 200ml (¾ cup) of water to the boil in a medium pan. Slice half the shiitake mushrooms and dice the other half. Add to the boiling water, give a good stir for 20 seconds, then drain into a colander. Leave for 30 seconds, then tip into a bowl and mix in the miso dressing. Cover with cling film (plastic wrap) and leave to marinate, stirring again after 10 minutes.

Snap the ends from the asparagus and peel the lower 3cm (1¼in.). Blanch in salted boiling water, or steam, for 1½ minutes, then refresh in iced water. Drain.

To serve, toss the asparagus and salad leaves with the lemon juice and lay them on your plates. Spoon on the mushrooms and marinating juices, then tuck in the quail eggs and scatter with the almonds.

Patty-pan squash, roast olives and potatoes, girolles and sherry-vinegar currants

WARM OR AT ROOM TEMPERATURE

When wild mushrooms are in season, there's no excuse not to put them in everything and anything savoury. The best mushrooms in the market the day we shot this were girolles, but you can replace them with any wild mushroom. If you can't get wild ones, cultivated oyster mushrooms or shiitake, or even chestnut mushrooms, work well. You can even supplement fresh mushrooms with dried ones for variety – you'll just need to soak and rinse them to ensure no grit ends up in your meal. I love the flying-saucer-shaped patty-pan squash, which are becoming more common, but use courgettes (zucchini) if you can't get them. Serve as a starter or as an accompaniment to a main course.

INGREDIENTS

2 tbsp currants

2 tbsp sherry vinegar

500g (1lb. 2oz.) baby potatoes or small waxy potatoes, halved

4 garlic cloves, thickly sliced

200g (7oz./1 cup) mixed olives

1 tsp cumin seeds

½ tsp fennel seeds

½ tsp smoked paprika

1 tsp thyme

2 tbsp olive oil

500g (1lb. 2oz.) patty-pan squash, stalks removed

30g (1oz./2 tbsp) butter

8 sage leaves, torn

150g (5½oz.) girolle mushrooms, brushed

100g (3½oz.) baby salad leaves (I used spinach and kale)

[METHOD]

Preheat the oven to 170°C (350°F/Gas mark 4).

Put the currants in a small pan with the sherry vinegar and 2 tablespoons of water. Place on a medium heat and bring to the boil. Put a lid on, cook for 2 minutes, then turn off the heat and leave to one side.

Put the potatoes and garlic in a pan, cover with water, add 1 teaspoon of fine salt and bring to the boil. Cook for 5 minutes, then drain into a colander. Tip into a roasting dish with the olives, cumin and fennel seeds, smoked paprika, thyme, olive oil and 1 teaspoon of flaky salt. Cut 1 or 2 of the squash into wedges and add to the dish. Roast for about 25 minutes until the potatoes are cooked and coloured, stirring several times. (Slightly overcooking the potatoes works well.)

Slice the remaining squash 5mm (¼in.) thick and blanch in boiling salted water (or steam) for 2 minutes, then drain and leave to one side.

Heat the butter in a frying pan (skillet) until sizzling, then add the sage and mushrooms. Cook over a medium heat, gently stirring from time to time, until the mushrooms collapse and soften. Add the currants and the soaking liquid. Season with salt and coarsely ground black pepper.

To serve, mix the baby salad leaves and blanched squash into the hot potatoes and divide among your plates. Spoon on the mushrooms.

Kohlrabi, watermelon, tofu, mangetout, curry leaves and candied walnuts

AT ROOM TEMPERATURE

INGREDIENTS

100g (3½oz./1 cup) walnut halves

50g (1¾oz./¼ cup) dark 'molasses' sugar (muscovado, brown or Demerara, or use a dark honey or treacle)

oil for deep-frying

350g (12oz.) silken tofu

2 tbsp cornflour (cornstarch; or use rice flour or wheat flour)

3 tbsp curry leaves, taken off the stem

1 medium kohlrabi (300g/10½oz.), peeled and thinly shredded or julienned

1kg (2lb. 4oz.) chunk watermelon, skin removed to give you about 700g (1lb. 9oz.) flesh, cut into cubes

100g (3½oz.) mangetout (snow peas), blanched, refreshed and sliced diagonally into thirds

2 tbsp snipped dill

2 tbsp lemon juice

3 tbsp extra virgin olive oil

Kohlrabi is a most peculiar-looking vegetable that I remember eating as a child (my grandmother was a terrific gardener and grew them). Then, we always had them steamed and tossed with butter, but in fact they are even better raw as they're nice and crunchy. This process of candying the walnuts is really worth the effort, but if you don't have time, you can replace them with toasted nuts – although they keep for 2 weeks in a sealed jar so you can make them in advance. If you can't get curry leaves, use parsley or basil leaves instead, but they will cook much more quickly, so keep an eye on them so they don't burn.

[METHOD]

Place the walnuts in a saucepan and cover with water. Bring to the boil, cook for 1 minute, then drain into a sieve and rinse. Place back in the saucepan and add enough water to cover by 3cm (1¼in.). Add the sugar, bring to the boil then reduce to a rapid simmer and cook, stirring frequently, until you have only 1cm (½in.) of liquid left in the bottom. Drain into a sieve. Transfer to a baking sheet lined with non-stick baking parchment and leave to dry at room temperature overnight.

Next day, heat the oven to 140°C (275°F/Gas mark 1). Lift the nuts off the baking parchment – if any are so stuck they don't come off easily then you will need to place all the nuts on a fresh sheet of parchment. Bake in the oven for 25 minutes, at which point they will be sticky and beginning to colour. Give them a toss half-way through. Once the stickiness lessens, increase the oven temperature to 160°C (325°F/Gas mark 3) and continue to cook until they begin to smell toasty, about another 15 minutes. Turn off the oven and leave them to cool in there, then remove from the baking sheet, separate the nuts if stuck together, and store in an airtight container. If they appear at all moist, cook them for a while longer.

Pour vegetable oil into a wok or saucepan to a depth of 5cm (2in.) and heat to 180°C (350°F). Cut the tofu into cubes, lay it on absorbent kitchen paper, then gently press more kitchen paper on top. (This draws out excess moisture so they will splatter less when deep-fried.) Leave for 5 minutes, then place in a dish and sprinkle it with the cornflour (cornstarch), gently tossing it to coat it, then shaking off the excess. Carefully lower half the tofu into the oil, spacing the cubes well apart so they don't stick together. Deep-fry until golden, gently moving them around in the oil. Place onto absorbent kitchen paper to drain and cook the remaining tofu.

Once all the tofu is cooked, turn off the heat and leave the oil to cool for 3 minutes. Add the curry leaves to the oil, which will sizzle and splatter a little, stir them around and remove with a slotted spoon onto absorbent kitchen paper once the sizzling stops.

To serve, toss the tofu, kohlrabi, watermelon, mangetout (snow peas), dill, lemon juice and olive oil together with flaky salt to taste. Divide among your plates and scatter with the curry leaves and walnuts.

Leeks vinaigrette, salt-baked carrots and parsnips, tarragon and sunflower seeds

AT ROOM TEMPERATURE

INGREDIENTS

800g (1lb. 12oz.) leeks (about 4 medium)

3 tbsp mustard (I used a mixture of English and grain)

3 tbsp white vinegar (cider, white wine or rice vinegar)

75ml (5 tbsp) sunflower or light olive oil

600g (1lb. 5oz.) carrots (4 or 5; I used a variety of colours)

300g (10½oz.) parsnips (about 3)

6 thyme sprigs (or 1 tsp leaves)

2 tsp rosemary leaves

4 garlic cloves, sliced

500g (1lb. 2oz./2⅔ cups) coarse salt

2 tarragon sprigs, leaves removed from stem

3 tbsp sunflower seeds, toasted

I vividly recall eating leeks vinaigrette for the first time at Père Lachaise cemetery in Paris in 1996. I was off to find the tombs of Oscar Wilde, Edith Piaf and Chopin and had stopped in a deli to get some rillettes and bread, and bought these marinated leeks. I fell in love with them then and there. The salt-baked carrots and parsnips are very 'on trend', although, like me, you may have been baking whole fish in a salt crust for years and not even have known that you were ahead of the game. Oddly, they become very savoury, but not overly salty, when cooked this way – provided you don't tear the skin, which will let the salt enter their flesh.

[METHOD]

Ideally, cook the leeks 12 hours before you plan to eat this. Trim them, cutting the base off just above the roots. Cut the leaves off where they begin to open out and where the grit and soil gets in. These green parts can be used for something else (stocks, soups, casseroles, etc.), but they don't work well here. Remove any outer leaves that are damaged and wash well to remove any soil. You should have about 600g (1lb. 5oz.) left. Cut into 10–15cm (4–6in.) lengths. Steam or boil in salted water until you can just insert a sharp knife through the centre, about 9 minutes. Carefully remove with tongs and drain for 1 minute in a colander.

While the leeks are cooking, make the mustard vinaigrette. Whisk the mustard and vinegar with 1 teaspoon of salt and ¼ teaspoon of coarsely ground black pepper, then whisk in the oil.

Put the drained, still-hot leeks into a non-reactive dish just large enough to hold them. Pour the mustard vinaigrette over them, turning after an hour. Once cooled, store in the fridge. Leave for at least 12 hours to marinate.

Preheat the oven to 190°C (375°C/Gas mark 5).

Lightly rub off any soil from the carrots and parsnips but avoid breaking their skin. Mix the thyme, rosemary, garlic and salt together and place a quarter of the mixture in the bottom of a baking dish just large enough to hold the carrots and parsnips in a single layer. Lay the vegetables on top and then cover with the remaining salt, patting it evenly. Bake in the oven until you can insert a sharp knife through the carrots, which will take about 40 minutes depending on the size of your vegetables. Leave to cool until you can handle them. Pull the carrots and parsnips out of the salt, wiping excess away, then rub off any skin that you're able to. Top and tail, then cut into thick slices.

To serve, lay the leeks and root vegetables on your plates and spoon over the mustard marinade. Scatter on the tarragon leaves and sunflower seeds.

FOR 4 AS A BRUNCH DISH

Crusty baked wasabi mushrooms, spinach, tomato, orange, dill and grated egg

WARM OR AT ROOM TEMPERATURE

INGREDIENTS

8 portabella mushrooms (about 600g/1lb. 5oz.)

70g (2½oz./⅓ cup) butter

2 garlic cloves, finely chopped

½ tsp finely chopped rosemary

1½ tsp wasabi paste (more or less to taste)

150g (5½oz./2½ cups fresh) coarse white breadcrumbs (or use Japanese panko crumbs)

3 large tomatoes, blanched and peeled

2 oranges, peeled and pith removed, segments removed and any juice saved

3 tbsp coarsely shredded dill

1 tbsp extra virgin olive oil

150g (5½oz.) baby spinach or other baby salad leaf

4 large free-range eggs, soft boiled and peeled

As a child I'd only ever eaten big open field mushrooms sliced and fried in butter or grilled on the barbecue after we'd harvested them ourselves. My father, Bruce, would drive our huge caramel-brown Chevrolet Impala car slowly across various farmers' fields and me and my siblings would lie on our bellies behind the front seat, with our heads, shoulders and arms out of the car, and pull them out of the ground. Hilarious, when I think about it – thankfully, dad was a very safe driver! If you don't have wasabi to hand, then you can replace it with mustard or horseradish. It's worth the effort to peel the tomatoes for this salsa, but, of course, if you're short of time you can skip this.

[METHOD]

Preheat the oven to 170°C (350°F/Gas mark 4). If the mushrooms have thick stalks, then cut them out and thinly slice. If they have a thick skin, you may want to peel them. Lay the mushrooms in one or two baking dishes, open side facing up. Heat the butter in a frying pan (skillet) over a medium heat with the garlic, rosemary and sliced mushroom stalks (if using) and cook until the garlic turns golden, stirring frequently. Remove the pan from the heat. Mix the wasabi paste with 1 tablespoon of water to form a slurry and stir into the butter. Stir in the breadcrumbs thoroughly. Spoon this mixture on top of the mushrooms and bake until the crumbs are golden, about 20 minutes.

Cut the tomatoes in half crossways and gently squeeze out the seeds, or use a teaspoon to scoop them out. Cut the tomato flesh into chunks and mix with the orange segments and juice. Add the dill and olive oil, season with salt and coarse black pepper and stir together.

To serve, divide the spinach among your plates and sit the mushrooms on top. Spoon on the tomato and orange and then, using a coarse grater, grate the eggs over the top.

Cherry, cherry tomato, orange, fennel, macadamia nuts and coriander

AT ROOM TEMPERATURE

INGREDIENTS

300g (10½oz./2¼ cups) cherries, pitted and halved

400g (14oz.) cherry tomatoes, halved

1 orange, peel and pith removed

2 heads fennel, trimmed (about 500g/1lb. 2oz.)

2 tbsp extra virgin olive oil

50g (1¾oz./⅓ cup) macadamia nuts, toasted

¼ tsp fennel seeds, lightly toasted

2 handfuls baby spinach leaves (or other salad leaves)

1 small handful coriander (cilantro), leaves picked off and stalks thinly sliced

It's important for the cherries to be really sweet and ripe otherwise the highlights of this salad will be less noticeable, so save this dish for summer. I love the butteriness of macadamia nuts, but you could replace them with cashews, almonds or pine nuts. This also works well as a main course if you serve it with a poached chicken breast (fillet), steamed fish or thickly sliced grilled (broiled) aubergine (eggplant) scattered with feta.

[METHOD]

Place the cherries and cherry tomatoes in a large bowl.

Cut the segments from the orange and cut each in half. Add to the cherries, along with the squeezed juice from the orange membrane.

Slice the fennel as thin as you can, crossways, and add to the cherries. Add the olive oil and ½ teaspoon of flaky salt.

Pound the macadamia nuts and fennel seeds roughly with a mortar and pestle.

To serve, add the spinach and coriander (cilantro) stalks to the cherry mixture and toss it all together. Put it all on a platter or divide among your plates and scatter with the crushed macadamia nuts and fennel seeds and the coriander (cilantro) leaves.

FOR 8 AS A STARTER OR A SIDE DISH

Green papaya, green mango, chilli, coconut, lime and tofu

SLIGHTLY CHILLED OR AT ROOM TEMPERATURE

INGREDIENTS

4 tbsp pale palm sugar, grated (or use unrefined caster/superfine or demerara sugar)

2 tsp finely grated lime zest

2 garlic cloves, finely chopped

120ml (½ cup) lime juice

350g (12oz.) silken tofu (if you use firm tofu you'll need to grate it finely)

1 medium bunch coriander (cilantro), leaves shredded and stalks chopped (if it has roots attached, wash to remove dirt, chop finely and use these too – they have a delicious flavour)

1 x 500g (1lb. 2oz.) green papaya, peeled, halved, deseeded and julienned

2 green mangos, peeled, flesh removed and shredded or julienned

2 medium-heat green chillies, finely chopped (more or less to taste, but heat is good here)

2 spring onions (scallions), thinly sliced

40 mint leaves, shredded

100g (3½oz.) coconut flesh, coarsely grated and lightly toasted (1⅓ cups grated)

This is a really refreshing salad to have as a first course or part of a main meal, but it's equally good served with sliced raw fish on top, alongside cold poached chicken or roast duck or even with ham. You can buy green papaya and green mangos from Southeast Asian food stores, but they can be replaced with crunchy vegetables like kohlrabi, celeriac, cucumbers (small ones tend to be crunchier) or even apples and nashi pears. Green papayas come in varying sizes but if you use a little more or less here it won't affect the salad alarmingly. A mandolin is great for julienning these. If you can't access a whole coconut, then buy long-thread desiccated (shredded) coconut or coconut chips instead. If you're not vegetarian, try seasoning this with fish sauce instead of salt – the flavour is fabulous!

[METHOD]

Make the dressing. Using a mortar and pestle, pound the palm sugar with the lime zest and garlic and 2 tablespoons of the lime juice until the sugar dissolves. Holding the tofu in your hand, squash it out between your fingers into the mortar, then mix in the remaining lime juice. Mix in half the coriander (cilantro) and leave at room temperature.

In a large bowl, mix together the remaining coriander (cilantro), the papaya, mango, chillies, spring onions (scallions) and mint. Add a third of the tofu dressing and toss it all together. Taste for seasoning, adding salt to taste.

To serve, divide the salad among your plates. Spoon on the remaining tofu dressing and sprinkle with the coconut.

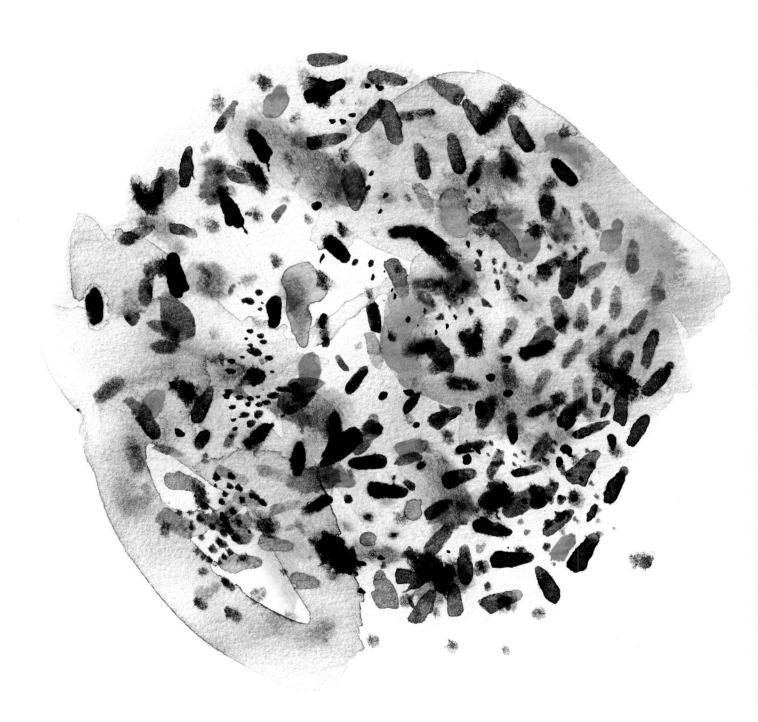

Veggie Grains

CHAPTER 3

FOR 4 AS A STARTER OR 6–8 AS A SIDE DISH

Aubergine, quinoa, gem lettuce, tomato and pistachio

AT ROOM TEMPERATURE

INGREDIENTS

1 large aubergine (eggplant) (about 450g/1lb.)

75ml (5 tbsp) olive oil

1 lemon

250g (9oz./1½ cups) quinoa, rinsed and drained

2 gem lettuces

1 medium bunch coriander (cilantro), on the stalk, a few leaves saved for garnish, the rest shredded

1 tbsp balsamic vinegar

2 tbsp grain mustard

3 tomatoes (about 350g/12oz.), diced

100g (3½oz./⅔ cup) pistachio nuts, lightly toasted

Quinoa is a very versatile grain to use because, like millet, it doesn't need much cooking and is therefore easy to add to your meal. It's also highly nutritious. For this recipe I used a mixture of red and white quinoa, which looks good. Choose a variety of tomatoes, for their colour and shape, and vary the salad leaves, too, if you prefer.

[METHOD]

Cut the stalk from the aubergine (eggplant) and slice it lengthways into six. Stack half of these slices on top of each other on a chopping board and cut them lengthways again into six long batons (per slice). Repeat with the other three slices. Lay the batons on a baking sheet or in a roasting dish, drizzle with 3 tablespoons of olive oil and season with salt. Place under a grill (broiler) and cook until golden, turning them several times. They're done when soft enough to almost squeeze between your fingers. Take from the grill (broiler) and leave to cool. As they're cooling, grate the zest from half the lemon over and season lightly with salt and pepper.

Bring 1 litre (4¼ cups) of water to the boil in a large pan and add the quinoa. Cook for 9–12 minutes, by which point the quinoa will still have a little bite but will have softened in texture. Drain in a fine sieve and leave to cool.

Trim the base from the gem lettuces and discard the outer leaves if blemished. Separate, wash and drain the leaves.

Mix the juice from the lemon with the remaining 2 tablespoons of olive oil, the balsamic vinegar, mustard and a little salt.

To serve, toss everything except the dressing and the nuts together and place on a platter. Spoon on the dressing, then scatter with the nuts.

Quinoa, poached tofu and shiitake, roast beetroot, wasabi, endive, crispy capers and curry leaves

AT ROOM TEMPERATURE

INGREDIENTS

300g (10½oz.) baby beetroot (beets), skins gently washed and scrubbed if dirty (if you're using whole bunches with leaves attached, then buy about 700g/1lb. 9oz.)

½ tsp finely grated orange zest

1 tbsp orange juice

1–2 tsp wasabi paste

1 tbsp extra virgin olive oil

vegetable oil for deep-frying

1 tbsp salted (or brined) capers, rinsed and patted dry

20 curry leaves

200g (7oz./1¼ cups) quinoa

5cm (2in.) piece ginger, peeled and thinly sliced

2 tbsp soy sauce

300g (10½oz.) silken tofu, cut into 1.5cm (½in.) cubes

100g (3½oz.) shiitake mushrooms, stems discarded, caps cut into wedges

2 heads endive (chicory), leaves separated, washed and drained

Poaching, or steaming, tofu gives it a lovely texture. Use a silken tofu rather than a firm yellow tofu as the end result is much nicer for this salad. If you can't find fresh silken tofu, then you can buy it in a tetra-pak as quality is generally good; these are usually about 300–350g (10½–12oz.), so simply use one packet. Ideally, buy beetroot (beets) with their leaves still on as they'll be fresher and the leaves are edible, cooked in the same way as spinach. If you're unable to deep-fry the various components, buy beetroot (beet) reggie crisps (chips) and serve the capers rinsed and patted dry. Use shredded flat-leaf (Italian) parsley, mint or basil leaves instead of the crispy curry leaves; although they're not the same, they make a pretty good substitute.

[METHOD]

Preheat the oven to 190°C (375°C/Gas mark 5). Wrap all but one of the beetroot (beets) in a double layer of foil, like a parcel, and bake until you can easily insert a skewer through the foil from one side of a beetroot (beet) to the other. For golf-ball-sized beetroot (beets), this will take about 40 minutes.

Remove from the oven and leave to cool, then peel the skin off (wear gloves to prevent your hands from staining if using red beets like I did). Cut into 5mm (¼in.) slices and mix with the orange zest and juice, wasabi and olive oil.

Heat 3cm (1¼in.) of vegetable oil in a medium pan to 160°C (325°F). Peel and slice the reserved beetroot (beet) as thin as you can into rounds (a mandolin is good for this). Add half the beetroot (beet) slices, one at a time to prevent them sticking to each other, and deep-fry, gently turning them as they cook, until crisp. Remove with a slotted spoon and drain on absorbent kitchen paper. Lightly season with salt while warm, and cook the remainder. Add the capers and fry until golden and crisp. Remove from the hot oil with a slotted spoon and drain on kitchen paper. Fry the curry leaves in the same way, drain and reserve.

To cook the quinoa, half-fill a medium pan with water and bring to the boil. Rinse the quinoa in a fine sieve under hot running water for 15 seconds (this will remove

[RECIPE CONTINUES]

[RECIPE CONTINUED]

some of the grain's bitterness), then add to the boiling water. Cook for 9–12 minutes: it should have softened but still have a little bite. Drain in a fine sieve and leave to cool.

Put the ginger and soy in a medium saucepan with 500ml (2 cups) of water and bring to a gentle boil. Carefully add the diced tofu to the boiling liquid along with the shiitake mushrooms. Bring back almost to the boil, then reduce the heat to a gentle simmer and poach for 3 minutes with the lid on, giving it a gentle stir half-way through. Turn off the heat and leave to cool in the liquid for 15 minutes. Gently tip into a colander and drain. The poaching liquor can be saved, cooled and frozen to be used in a stock at a later date.

To serve, toss the quinoa with the endive (chicory) leaves and salt to taste. Lay the marinated beetroot (beet) slices on top along with the marinating liquid. Scatter over the tofu, shiitake and ginger, then top with the beetroot (beet) crisps (chips), capers and curry leaves.

FOR 6 AS A STARTER

Chickpeas, grilled broccoli and asparagus with popped chilli grapes and bagel croutons

AT ROOM TEMPERATURE

INGREDIENTS

175g (6oz./¾ cup + 2 tbsp) dried chickpeas

2 tsp baking soda

1 bay leaf (or use a few fresh thyme, oregano or rosemary sprigs)

85ml (⅓ cup) Greek-style plain yogurt

2 bagels, slightly stale (or use 3 slices of bread, cut into 2cm/¾in. squares)

2 tbsp + 1 tsp extra virgin olive oil

200g (7oz./2 cups) black and green grapes

½ medium-heat red chilli, finely chopped, including the seeds (more or less to taste)

3 tbsp verjus (or use 2 tbsp cider vinegar or rice wine vinegar plus 1 tbsp water)

250g (9oz.) broccoli (about 1 head)

600g (1lb. 5oz.) asparagus (about 300g/10½oz. trimmed weight, see method)

1 small handful watercress, mâche (corn salad) or rocket (arugula) leaves

20 mint leaves, torn

Chickpeas are incredibly easy to cook from dried but you will need to soak them overnight in water and baking soda before cooking them, so if time isn't on your side you can resort to canned ones. I used broccoli and asparagus in this dish because they were in season when we shot the photograph, but you can also use sweetcorn, pumpkin, carrots, aubergine (eggplant) or other vegetables instead. The bagel croutons add a lovely chewiness and crunch to the salad, so if you're gluten intolerant, use gluten-free bread rather than leave them out. This salad can be served as a first course, or as part of a meal.

[METHOD]

First cook the chickpeas, which you'll need to begin the day before. Put them into a large bowl with the baking soda and cover with 1 litre (4¼ cups) of cold water. Cover with cling film (plastic wrap) and leave for 12 hours to rehydrate. Drain and rinse well under cold water. Place in a medium pan and pour over 1 litre (4¼ cups) of water, then slowly bring to the boil and skim off any foam that rises to the surface. Reduce the heat to a gentle boil, skim off any more foam, then add the bay leaf and cook for 30–45 minutes, depending on the size of the chickpeas. Make sure that they remain covered by at least 1cm (½in.) of water. To test if they're cooked, try one after 30 minutes. Drain into a colander and briefly rinse under cold water. Drain again, then place in a bowl with the yogurt. Add ½ teaspoon of salt and some freshly milled black pepper and mix it all together.

To make the croutons, preheat the oven to 160°C (325°F/Gas mark 3). Cut the bagels into slices 5mm (¼in.) thick, toss with 1 tablespoon of the olive oil and lay on a baking sheet. Bake until golden and crisp, turning the slices over after 15 minutes. Once cooked, remove from the oven and leave to cool. Store in an airtight container for up to a week.

To pop the grapes, put them in a medium pan with 2 teaspoons of olive oil and place over a medium heat. Cook until they begin to blister, stirring them gently as they heat up. Once most have popped their skins a little, add the chilli and verjus

[RECIPE CONTINUES]

[RECIPE CONTINUED]

and 2 pinches of salt. Bring to the boil, then put a lid on the pan, turn off the heat and leave to cool down.

Cut the broccoli into florets, keeping as much stalk intact as possible. Blanch for no more than a minute in lightly salted boiling water. Drain, refresh in iced water and drain again. Place in a bowl.

To prepare the asparagus, snap the stalk ends off where they naturally break – this will be where the fibrous and woody part starts. Use a vegetable peeler to remove the lower 5cm (2in.) of peel. Mix the asparagus with the blanched broccoli and toss with 2 teaspoons of the oil.

Place a heavy-based frying pan (skillet) over a high heat and cook the asparagus and broccoli until coloured, turning them as they cook, then remove to a plate to cool. Slice the asparagus spears in half on an angle.

To serve, place the salad leaves on your plates and lay the broccoli and asparagus on top. Stir the mint into the chickpeas, then spoon these on. Scatter with the croutons and spoon on the grapes and their juices.

Puy lentils, quinoa, pomegranate-roast grapes and tomatoes, chilli, mint and basil

WARM OR AT ROOM TEMPERATURE

INGREDIENTS

200g (7oz./2 cups) black and green grapes

200g (7oz.) cherry tomatoes (use several colours)

1 banana shallot, thinly sliced

½ medium-heat red chilli, including the seeds, chopped

2 tbsp pomegranate molasses

4 tbsp extra virgin olive oil

200g (7oz./1 cup) puy lentils, rinsed and drained

4 garlic cloves, sliced

1 tsp finely chopped thyme leaves

1 tsp finely chopped rosemary leaves

1 tsp finely chopped oregano leaves

1 bay leaf

150g (5½oz./scant 1 cup) quinoa, rinsed and drained

1 handful parsley leaves

30 mint leaves

20 basil leaves

A warm salad that also has the benefit of being a double-grainer, this has got to be good for you! I adore lentils for their slightly pasty texture; they have a really earthy yet light flavour and they can be cooked relatively quickly compared with things like chickpeas or butter (lima) beans. I've teamed lentils with quinoa, which is a very light grain (see page 75) and even quicker to cook. Roasting the grapes and tomatoes together works well, particularly if you use as many different colours as possible, and the juices become part of the dressing, drizzled over the finished salad. You can also make this in advance and serve at room temperature.

[METHOD]

Preheat the oven to 170°C (350°F/Gas mark 4).

Put the grapes, cherry tomatoes, shallot, chilli, pomegranate molasses and 2 tablespoons of the olive oil in a roasting dish with a little salt and pepper. Stir together, then bake until the grapes and cherry tomatoes have popped a little, about 30 minutes or so. Keep warm.

Meanwhile, cook the lentils. Put them in a medium saucepan and pour on enough water to cover the lentils by 4cm (1½in.). Bring to the boil, skimming any foam that rises off the surface. Reduce the heat to a rapid simmer, then stir in the garlic, thyme, rosemary, oregano, bay leaf and the remaining 2 tablespoons of olive oil. Put a lid on the pan and cook for 30 minutes, adding 1 teaspoon of flaky salt in the last 10 minutes. Don't let the water level fall below the surface of the lentils: top up with a little boiling water if needed. Taste a lentil to make sure they're done. Keep warm.

When the lentils have been cooking for about 15 minutes, cook the quinoa (see page 75).

To serve, toss the lentils and quinoa with the parsley and mint. Taste for seasoning. Mix the basil gently into the grapes and sit this on top, then drizzle with the roasting juices.

INGREDIENTS

1 cinnamon stick

3 star anise

5cm (2in.) piece ginger, peeled and thinly sliced

½ red chilli, sliced

250ml (1 cup) red wine

100g (3½oz./½ cup) sugar (or use honey or maple syrup)

2 bay leaves

200g (7oz.) vacuum-packed chestnuts, rinsed and drained

4 firm, ripe pears

250g (9oz./1¼ cups) green lentils, rinsed and drained

75ml (5 tbsp) olive oil

4 garlic cloves, chopped

1 tbsp chopped mixed fresh hard herbs (thyme, rosemary, sage, oregano)

2 red onions, halved and thinly sliced

50g (1¾oz./⅓ cup) currants

3 tbsp sherry vinegar or balsamic vinegar

1 head broccoli, cut into florets

FOR 6–8 AS A STARTER OR SIDE DISH

Green lentils, poached pear and chestnuts, broccoli, caramelized onions and currants

WARM OR AT ROOM TEMPERATURE

This is a lovely autumn (fall) or winter salad that you could also top with crumbled semi-firm cheese or grated (shredded) Comté cheese. The chestnuts I used were vacuum packed and are available all year round, but there's nothing better than freshly roasted ones if they're available. Puy lentils work well here in place of the green lentils, but you could also use bulgur wheat or pearl barley.

[METHOD]

Put the cinnamon stick, star anise, ginger, chilli, red wine, sugar, 1 bay leaf and ¼ teaspoon of salt into a medium pan. Pour in 700ml (3 cups) of water and bring to the boil, then reduce the heat to a simmer and add the chestnuts. Peel the pears, cut in half lengthways and remove the core. Place in the poaching liquid and top up with more boiling water, if needed, to cover them. Bring back to the boil, then reduce the heat to a rapid simmer. Place a paper cartouche, with a hole in the centre, on top of the liquid and cook for 40 minutes. Leave to cool.

Meanwhile, cook the lentils. Heat 2 tablespoons of the oil in a medium pan with the garlic, herbs and remaining bay leaf. Once the garlic turns golden, add the lentils, 700ml (3 cups) of water and 1 teaspoon of salt. Bring to the boil, then reduce the heat to a rapid simmer and cook, covered, until done, about 20–25 minutes. Leave in the pan to keep warm.

Meanwhile, heat the remaining 3 tablespoons of oil in a pan on a medium heat and sauté the onions and ½ teaspoon of salt with the lid on until they collapse and begin to caramelize, about 15 minutes, stirring occasionally. Remove the lid, add the currants and cook for a further 3 minutes, stirring to prevent them burning. Add the vinegar and cook, stirring, for 2 minutes to reduce the liquid. Keep warm.

Blanch the broccoli in salted boiling water for 2 minutes, then drain.

Just before serving, remove the pears and chestnuts from their poaching liquid and slice the pears. To serve, toss the lentils and broccoli together and divide among your plates. Lay the sliced pear and chestnuts on top with the sliced chilli from the poaching liquid, then spoon on the caramelized onions and currants.

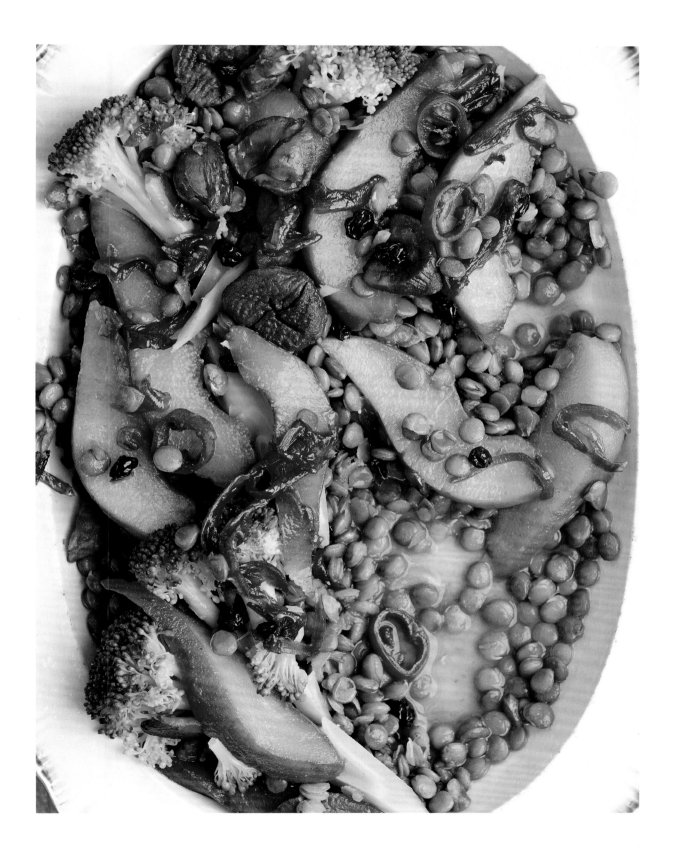

FOR 6—8 AS A SIDE DISH

Fregola, asparagus, shiitake mushrooms and walnuts

WARM OR AT ROOM TEMPERATURE

INGREDIENTS

200g (7oz./1 cup) fregola, rinsed and drained

3 tbsp olive oil

1 red onion, thinly sliced

2 garlic cloves, thinly sliced

10 fresh shiitake mushrooms, stalks removed and discarded, caps quartered

2 tsp fresh thyme leaves

800g (1lb. 12oz.) asparagus, ends snapped off and discarded (about 450g/1lb. trimmed weight)

20 cherry tomatoes, halved

1 handful fresh soft herbs (e.g. dill, fennel, mint, parsley, young oregano or marjoram, coriander/cilantro), roughly chopped or torn

2 tbsp lemon juice

60g (2¼oz./½ cup) walnuts, lightly toasted, roughly chopped

Although it's not a grain, fregola is made from wheat and so it kind of fits in here. Other, similar, versions are known as Israeli couscous, maftoul or mograbiah. Some simply look like white balls of dried pasta dough, some are uneven in shape and some are toasted. In my mind, the key to a flavoursome dish using any of these is always to toast the fregola (if it's not already toasted) before boiling it, either by frying in oil, as here, or dry toasting it in the oven. Alternatively, you could use orzo, the Greek rice-shaped pasta. I'm a big fan of both.

[METHOD]

To cook the fregola, place a medium pan over a medium heat and sauté the fregola in half the oil until golden in colour, stirring frequently. If it's already toasted, sauté for just a minute. Add the onion, garlic and shiitake, and fry until the onion wilts, stirring constantly. Add the thyme and then, very slowly, add 800ml (3⅓ cups) of boiling water, standing back when you do so as steam can shoot out of the pan. Bring to the boil, then reduce the heat to a rapid simmer and cook with a lid on for 8 minutes. Taste a few grains: the fregola should be soft enough to bite into; if it's still too firm, keep cooking. If the water level has sunk below the top of the fregola, add a little more boiling water and keep cooking with the lid on. When it's ready, take the lid off and cook until the water has almost completely evaporated, stirring from time to time. Season with salt and pepper. Leave to cool in the pan or transfer to a large bowl.

While the fregola is cooking, blanch the asparagus briefly in lightly salted water. It's best a little crunchy when used in this dish, so 30 seconds will be plenty. Drain into a colander, then refresh in iced water for a few minutes if serving at room temperature. Drain again, then cut each spear on an angle into three pieces.

To serve, mix the asparagus, tomatoes, fresh herbs, lemon juice and remaining olive oil into the fregola. Taste for seasoning, then scatter on the walnuts.

Freekeh, cumin-roast artichoke, grilled corn and pomegranate

WARM OR AT ROOM TEMPERATURE

INGREDIENTS

1 large juicy lemon

2 bay leaves

4–6 large globe artichokes (1.5 kg/3lb. 5oz.) whole raw weight)

1 small red onion, finely chopped

3 garlic cloves, peeled and finely chopped

1 tsp cumin seeds

1 tsp fresh thyme, oregano or finely chopped rosemary

3 tbsp extra virgin olive oil

200g (7oz./1 cup) freekeh, rinsed and drained

2 corn cobs, husks removed

4 tbsp pumpkin seeds

1 whole pomegranate

20 mint leaves, torn

4 tbsp snipped dill (1–2cm/ ½–¾in. lengths)

2 handfuls wild rocket (arugula)

I love the smokiness of freekeh; it's quite unique in that way for a grain. I recall talking with a freekeh farmer in Turkey who explained why that is. At the end of summer, when the ground is dry and the grains are nearly ripe, but still with a little moisture in them, he sets fire to his fields. While the chaff and straw burn away, the grains, with their little amount of moisture, avoid incineration. They are then harvested and cracked, ready to be cooked. When cooking freekeh, I always add salt to the finished salad rather than to the water it's cooked in. In this book there are two ways to cook freekeh: here it is very simply boiled; the other way is to cook it more like a risotto (see page 97). Some recipes simply suit one style of cooking better than the other.

[METHOD]

Preheat the oven to 190°C (375°C/Gas mark 5).

First cook the artichokes. Pour water into a large saucepan until three quarters full, add 1 tablespoon of salt and bring to the boil. Slice half the lemon 5mm (¼in.) thick and add to the pan along with the bay leaves. Turn off the heat.

Holding an artichoke by its stalk, pull the thick leaves from the base of the head until you reach the leaves that are visibly thinner and softer. Then, laying the artichoke horizontally on a chopping board, cut off and discard the top two thirds using a sharp knife (a serrated one is good for this. Do be careful as the head can slide around a little and they can be a little tough). Cut off the stalk, near the base of the head, then trim off any rough edges using a small sharp knife. Using a teaspoon or a melon-baller, dig into the cavity of the artichoke to remove the hairy fibres, which are very unpleasant to eat. Place the prepared artichoke heart in the hot water and finish preparing the remaining ones. If the water doesn't cover them all, top up with boiling water. Bring the water back to a gentle boil. As you'll be roasting these, they only need to be par-cooked, so boil for just 5 minutes. Remove with a slotted spoon to a colander to drain and cool for 5 minutes. Discard the poaching liquid.

Cut each artichoke into quarters and place in a roasting dish with the onion, garlic, cumin, thyme and 1 tablespoon of the olive oil. Squeeze the remaining

[RECIPE CONTINUES]

[RECIPE CONTINUED]

half-lemon over them and season with salt and pepper. Toss well, then roast until golden and cooked through — about 20 minutes. Once cooked, remove from the oven and leave to cool — or use hot for a warm salad.

While the artichokes are roasting, pour water into another medium pan until three quarters full and bring to the boil. Add the freekeh and bring back to the boil. Lower the heat so that the water is at a rapid simmer and cook for 15 minutes. Taste a few grains — they should have a little bite to them, but also feel cooked. Drain into a sieve and leave to cool — unless you're making a warm salad.

While the freekeh is cooking, grill the corn. Put a heavy-based pan (skillet) on a medium–high heat until smoking hot. Brush the cobs with 1 teaspoon of olive oil and cook, turning them as they become golden brown. Once they're coloured all over, or near enough, remove from the pan and leave to cool on a plate. When cool enough to handle, cut the kernels from the cobs.

Put the pumpkin seeds and the remaining of olive oil in a small pan over a medium heat. The seeds will begin to pop and splash a little as they heat up. Once they begin to turn pale golden, tip them into a heatproof bowl and leave to cool.

Cut the pomegranate in half and remove the seeds from one of the halves, making sure you have no bitter white membrane attached. Squeeze the other half over a citrus juicer to extract the juice as you would an orange. It will likely splatter, so wear an apron, or stand well back.

To serve, toss the freekeh with the mint, dill and rocket (arugula), the pomegranate juice, half the corn, half the pomegranate seeds and 1 teaspoon of flaky salt. Spoon onto your plates. Lay the artichokes on top, along with the onions and oil from the roasting dish. Scatter over the remaining corn, the pomegranate seeds and the pumpkin seeds.

FOR 8 AS A STARTER OR SIDE DISH

Freekeh, walnut, Swiss chard, mushrooms and tahini mascarpone

WARM OR AT ROOM TEMPERATURE

INGREDIENTS

1 tbsp olive oil

1 red onion, thinly sliced

2 garlic cloves, thinly sliced

2 tbsp finely chopped or grated ginger

100g (3½oz./1 cup) walnuts, coarsely chopped

200g (7oz./1 cup) freekeh, rinsed and drained

1 tbsp cider vinegar

60g (2¼oz./¼ cup) butter

¾ medium-thickness leek, thinly sliced

4 portabella mushrooms (about 450g/1lb.), sliced

300g (10½oz.) Swiss chard

2 tbsp tahini

1 tbsp lemon juice

200g (7oz./scant 1 cup) mascarpone, at room temperature

1 small bunch flat-leaf (Italian) parsley (including stalks), coarsely chopped

This is another way to cook freekeh, instead of simply boiling it (see page 92); here it's cooked more like a rice pilaf. You can serve this either in one large bowl as part of a meal or as a starter. It goes well with a grilled (broiled) lamb neck chop or alongside a baked mackerel or a grilled (broiled) chunk of salmon. Use colourful rainbow chard if you can find it, and you could also use a variety of different mushrooms.

[METHOD]

First cook the freekeh. Heat a medium–large saucepan over a medium–high heat and add the olive oil. Add the onion, garlic and ginger and cook until caramelized, stirring often. Add the walnuts and cook for 30 seconds, coating them in the oil, then add the freekeh and 500ml (2 cups) of water. Bring to the boil, then cover the pan and lower the heat to a simmer. Add the freekeh and cook until it is almost cooked but still a little al dente, about 10–12 minutes. Turn off the heat, mix in the vinegar and 1 teaspoon of salt and leave to cool with the lid on.

While the freekeh is cooking, place a medium pan on a medium heat. Add the butter and cook until it turns nut brown. Add the leek and cook until it wilts, stirring as it cooks. Add the mushrooms and cook, stirring, until they, too, begin to collapse. Add salt to taste.

Next, prepare the Swiss chard. Cut the leaves from the stalks and wash both the leaves and stalks to remove any grit. Thinly slice the stalks crossways and put to one side. Roll up the leaves and shred them. Add the stalks to the mushroom mix and cook for 2 minutes, stirring from time to time. Stir in the leaves and taste for seasoning. Cover the pan and turn off the heat.

Mix the tahini and lemon juice together to a paste, then mix in the mascarpone until combined.

To serve, place the freekeh on your plates and spoon the mushroom and chard mixture on top. Dollop on the mascarpone and sprinkle with the parsley.

Bulgur, grilled carrots and broccoli, capers, pecans and lemon

WARM OR AT ROOM TEMPERATURE

INGREDIENTS

200g (7oz./scant 1 cup) bulgur wheat, rinsed and drained

3 carrots, peeled and sliced 5mm (¼in.) thick on an angle

500g (1lb. 2oz.) tender-stem broccoli, ends trimmed, cut in half lengthways

3 tbsp olive oil

2 tbsp pomegranate molasses

1 large lemon, peel and pith removed, pips discarded, flesh diced

30 mint leaves, shredded

60g (2¼oz./scant ⅔ cup) pecans, toasted and roughly chopped

1 tbsp capers, rinsed and patted dry

Bulgur is a wheat grain, which is steamed whole, then dried and broken into pieces. Because it has already been cooked, it is generally just soaked in boiling water. It comes in several grades, from fine to coarse, but medium works best here. Bulgur can be substituted with cracked wheat in this recipe, but it's worth pointing out that they're not the same thing: cracked wheat is made from dried uncooked wheat grains that have been crushed; they're generally larger pieces and they definitely need cooking – boil in plenty of lightly salted water for up to 30 minutes. The flavour is different, but not so much that you'll notice in this dish. If your lemon is a little on the sharp side, add half a teaspoon of caster (superfine) sugar to the vegetables.

[METHOD]

Put the bulgur in a large bowl and pour over 400ml (1⅔ cups) of boiling water. Stir in 1 teaspoon of salt. Cover the bowl with cling film (plastic wrap) or a tea (dish) towel and leave to soak for 30 minutes, stirring twice.

Meanwhile, bring a pan of salted water to the boil, then cook, separately, the carrots and then the broccoli, for 1 minute each. Drain and then toss the vegetables, again separately, in 2 teaspoons of olive oil each.

Heat a frying pan (skillet) or heavy-based pan and cook the vegetables until coloured and marked. Once cooked, place in a bowl and toss with the pomegranate molasses, lemon and remaining olive oil.

Drain the bulgur in a colander and leave for a few minutes. Place in a bowl with the mint, pecans and capers and toss well. Season with salt and pepper.

To serve, spread the bulgur out on a platter then lay the vegetables on top.

FOR 4 AS A LUNCHTIME DISH

Steamed ginger tempeh and aubergine, black rice, eggs and goji berries

WARM OR AT ROOM TEMPERATURE

INGREDIENTS

150g (5½oz./1 cup) black rice, soaked overnight in cold water, then rinsed and drained

2 tsp grated or finely chopped ginger

1 small shallot, diced

2 tbsp sesame oil

1½ tbsp soy sauce

2 tbsp lime juice

1 tbsp runny honey (or use maple syrup or agave syrup)

200g (7oz.) tempeh, cut into fat fingers or slabs

1 tbsp goji berries

1 aubergine (eggplant), stalk removed

1 handful watercress, trimmed and washed

4 eggs, soft boiled and peeled

1 small handful coriander (cilantro) leaves

1 spring onion (scallion), thinly sliced

I've been a lover of tofu and its more rustic and chunky, 'not-for-everyone', fermented sibling, tempeh, for as long as I can remember. When I was travelling through Southeast Asia in the early '80s, I recall tempeh being served in numerous dishes from gado gado to stir-fries and curries. If you can't get it, then by all means use a firm tofu here and reduce the cooking time by a few minutes. If you don't have time to soak the black rice overnight, just add extra water and an extra 15 minutes to the cooking time. This salad can be served warm or at room temperature and so makes a great lunchtime meal either in winter or in the middle of summer, and it's also a dish that makes you feel good and healthy!

[METHOD]

Put the rice in a medium saucepan and add 450ml (2 cups) of cold water. Bring to the boil, then put a lid on and cook on a very low simmer for 20 minutes. Taste a few grains: they should be al dente. If not, cook a little longer. Turn off the heat, mix in a little salt and set aside.

Mix the ginger, shallot, sesame oil, soy sauce, lime juice and honey together in a large bowl until the honey has dissolved.

Put a steamer on the hob (stove), add the tempeh and steam for 8 minutes. Scatter over the goji berries and steam for an additional 2 minutes. Add to the marinade and mix together.

Cut the aubergine (eggplant) into fat baton shapes and steam for 7–9 minutes until you can just squeeze them with your fingers (be careful – they'll be hot). Mix gently with the marinating tempeh and leave for 5 minutes.

To serve, spoon the rice and watercress onto your plates. Lay the tempeh mixture on then tuck in the eggs, cut in half. Scatter with the coriander (cilantro) and spring onions (scallions).

FOR 8 AS A SIDE DISH

Spelt, grilled radicchio, citrus, cashews, avocado and black radish

AT ROOM TEMPERATURE

INGREDIENTS

300g (10½oz./1½ cups) pearled spelt, rinsed and drained

1 large or 2 smaller heads radicchio, damaged outer leaves discarded, cut into 8–10 wedges if large or 4–6 if small

3 tbsp olive oil

1 pink grapefruit

2 satsumas (or clementines, mandarins or oranges), peeled, segmented and any pithy fibres and pips removed

2 avocados

200g (7oz.) black radish, lightly rinsed under cold water then thinly sliced (a mandolin is good for this)

125g (4½oz./generous ¾ cup) cashews, toasted and roughly chopped

Spelt has become very popular over the past decade but has been around forever. It's a member of the wheat family but appeals to people who see it as a more easily digestible 'grain'. However, it does contain gluten, so it's not for coeliacs. You can substitute pearled barley in this recipe but it will take an additional 20 minutes to cook. Pearling means the outer bran layer has been removed so it will cook quicker than if it hasn't been pearled. You can replace the radicchio with endive (chicory), halved lengthways (grilling/broiling it gives it a lovely toasty and sweetish flavour) and the black radish with regular red ones or thinly sliced daikon. This can be served as a side dish, or as a starter or main course with grilled (broiled) meat, or fish or goats' curd or blue cheese crumbled over it.

[METHOD]

First cook the spelt. Put it into a medium pan with 1 teaspoon of salt and cover with 3cm (1¼in.) of cold water. Bring to the boil, then cover the pan, reduce the heat to a rapid simmer and cook until tender, about 20 minutes. Drain in a colander and tip into a large bowl.

Cook the radicchio. Brush the cut sides with 1 tablespoon of the oil and sprinkle with a little salt. Place a heavy-based frying pan (skillet) or griddle on a medium–high heat. Cook the radicchio on both cut sides of the wedge until almost blackened. Remove from the heat and leave to cool. Cut out and discard the white core, then shred the leaves into fat ribbons and place in the bowl with the spelt.

Cut the top and bottom off the grapefruit, then cut the peel and pith off. Use a sharp knife to cut and separate the citrus segments away from the membrane that holds them in place and place in a separate bowl. Squeeze the juice from the membranes into the bowl as well – you'll get a few tablespoons of juice – and add the satsuma segments. Remove the flesh from the avocados, cut into wedges and add to the citrus, along with the sliced radish, remaining olive oil and half the cashews. Gently toss it all together.

To serve, gently toss the spelt and citrus salad together, then scatter with the remaining cashews.

Basmati saffron rice, butternut squash, tomato, cucumber and tamarind

WARM OR AT ROOM TEMPERATURE

INGREDIENTS

200g (7oz./1 cup) basmati rice, rinsed and drained

2 pinches saffron threads

2 tbsp vegetable oil

1 tsp mustard seeds

2 green cardamom pods, crushed flat, black seeds removed and husks discarded

5cm (2in.) cinnamon stick

20 curry leaves

600g (1lb. 5oz.) butternut squash, peeled and deseeded

1 red onion, thinly sliced

4 tomatoes

3 tbsp tamarind paste

½ tsp finely grated lime zest

2 tbsp lime juice

2 tsp sugar

1 small cucumber, thinly sliced

1 small bunch coriander (cilantro), leaves picked off, stalks cut into 5mm (¼in.) lengths

---

Basmati rice is a most delicious thing, but you can also use Thai Jasmine rice or flavoursome red Camargue rice, though you'll have less noticeable effect from the saffron in the latter. Tamarind paste ranges from very sour and sharp to more mellow. I always make my own by soaking tamarind pulp (a compressed brown and fibrous sticky mixture, available in Asian supermarkets) in warm water for 10 minutes, before breaking it up with my fingers and rubbing it through a coarse sieve. It's not always essential to peel tomatoes, but they do work better peeled for this recipe.

[METHOD]

Tip the rice into a bowl, cover with 600ml (2½ cups) of cold water and leave to soak for 30 minutes. Drain, then tip it back into the bowl, stir in the saffron and leave for 5 minutes.

Heat 1 teaspoon of the oil in a medium pan (with a tight-fitting lid) and add the mustard seeds. Cook until they pop, shaking the pan as they heat up. Add the cardamom seeds, cinnamon stick and curry leaves and sauté over a medium heat, stirring, until the curry leaves crispen a little (be careful not to burn the spices). Add the rice to the pan and mix it into the spices. Pour in 480ml (2 cups) of cold water and bring to the boil. Put the lid on and cook on the lowest heat for 11 minutes. Turn off the heat and leave for an additional 20 minutes. Remove the lid, sprinkle on ½ teaspoon of salt and give it a stir with a fork. If serving warm, keep in the saucepan; if serving at room temperature, tip into a bowl to cool.

While the rice is cooking, cook the butternut squash. Turn the oven to 180°C (350°F/Gas mark 4). Cut the squash into slices 1cm (½in.) thick and put in a roasting dish with the onion and 1 tablespoon of oil. Season with salt and pepper and toss together, then roast until the squash is cooked and coloured a little. Remove from the oven.

Peel the tomatoes. Pour water into a medium pan until three quarters full and bring to the boil. Using a sharp knife, score an X in the base of each tomato (cutting just the skin not the flesh). Have a bowl of iced water ready. Drop the tomatoes into the boiling water and leave for 30 seconds. Remove from the water with a slotted spoon and put into the iced water. Leave for 2 minutes, then peel off the skin. Cut the tomatoes in half crossways. Hold each half over a bowl, cut side down, and gently squeeze out and discard the seeds. Cut the flesh into chunks.

Make the dressing. Mix the tamarind paste with the lime zest and juice and sugar until the sugar has dissolved. Mix in the diced tomatoes, cucumber, coriander (cilantro) stalks and the remaining oil and ½ teaspoon of salt. Taste for seasoning.

To serve, spoon the rice on your plates and lay the squash on top. Spoon over the tomato salsa and scatter with the coriander (cilantro) leaves.

Millet, roast veggies, Pietro's egg and pomegranate

WARM

Millet is a quick-cooking grain that's easily digestible, light and gluten free. As a child, I used to feed stalks of millet to my budgies, Billy and Peach, so it took me a while to get my head around the fact that it isn't just birdseed! Like quinoa, which you could use in this salad instead of the millet, it's great added to salads almost as a bulking agent rather than as the main attraction. This technique of frying the eggs, which keeps the yolks runny, is courtesy of my hilarious friend Pietro, who divides his time between sunny Ibiza and Barcelona. Serve with lots of hot buttered crusty toast and grilled (broiled) chorizo if you like.

INGREDIENTS

2 carrots (I used an orange and a yellow one), peeled, ends cut off and sliced on an angle 5mm (¼in.) thick

1 fennel bulb, trimmed, thinly sliced lengthways

½ red onion, halved and thinly sliced

2 garlic cloves, sliced

½ medium-heat chilli (I used a green one, but red is also good), thinly sliced

85g (3oz./⅓ cup) butter

125g (4½oz./scant ⅔ cup) millet

about 150ml (⅔ cup) vegetable oil for frying the eggs

4 large eggs

100g (3½oz.) baby spinach leaves

4 tbsp pomegranate seeds

2 tbsp extra virgin olive oil

[METHOD]

Preheat the oven to 180°C (350°F/Gas mark 4). Put the carrots, fennel, onion, garlic and chilli in a roasting dish and toss together with a little salt and pepper. Dot on three quarters of the butter and roast in the oven, turning them once or twice while they cook, until golden, about 25 minutes. Keep warm.

While the vegetables are roasting, cook the millet. Half-fill a medium pan with water and bring to the boil. Meanwhile, dry-toast the millet in a frying pan (skillet) on a medium–high heat for 3½ minutes, shaking or stirring it several times to prevent it from catching. Tip the millet carefully into the boiling water and add the remaining butter and ½ teaspoon of salt. Cover the pan and cook on a low heat for 12 minutes. Taste a few grains: they should have a little bite. Drain the millet into a sieve, then return it to the pan, cover and keep warm.

To cook the eggs, it helps if you have a cardboard egg box to hand. Heat 7mm (¼in.) of vegetable oil in two medium (or one large) frying pans (skillets) until it gives off a shimmer of heat (at about 190°C/375°C/Gas mark 5). Crack open the eggs and tip their whites into four individual cups or ramekins. Put the yolks in their half-shells back in the egg box (to keep them upright). Carefully lower the whites into the hot oil and cook until they begin to crisp on the outside edges. Using a metal spoon, carefully spoon a little hot oil over the white to make it firm a little. Lower the yolks back onto the now semi-cooked whites. Drizzle a teaspoon of hot oil over the top of the yolk to help secure it, then remove from the pan.

To serve, toss the veggies, millet and spinach together and divide among warmed plates. Sit an egg on top, scatter with the pomegranate and drizzle with olive oil.

Farro, capers, herb-baked tomatoes, roast carrots and Parmesan

AT ROOM TEMPERATURE

Farro is a grain that has got a lot of attention in recent years as grains have become more commonplace and more nutritionally valued. I enjoy its texture and use it in salads such as this, but also serve it mixed with chopped roast cauliflower tossed with tahini and yogurt, or mixed into raw minced (ground) beef or lamb to make patties for the barbecue. Roast tomatoes are great at the height of summer when cooking makes them even sweeter, while in cooler months roasting will improve the flavour of hothouse-raised ones.

INGREDIENTS

300g (10½oz./1½ cups) farro, rinsed and drained

½ onion, chopped

1 bay leaf

3 tbsp baby capers

2 tbsp red wine vinegar

3 carrots (I used orange and purple ones), peeled and tops cut off, halved lengthways

4 tbsp extra virgin olive oil

1 tsp fresh thyme leaves

6 plum tomatoes, halved lengthways

1 tsp roughly chopped oregano

½ tsp chopped rosemary

2 handfuls rocket (arugula)

50g (1¾oz.) Parmesan, shaved with a sharp knife

[METHOD]

Preheat the oven to 170°C (350°F/Gas mark 4).

First cook the farro. Put it into a medium pan, cover with 3cm (1¼in.) of cold water and add the onion and bay leaf. Bring to the boil and put a lid on the pan. Reduce the heat to a rapid simmer and cook until the grains are tender, about 40 minutes. Add 1 teaspoon of flaky salt after 20 minutes. Drain in a colander, then transfer to a large bowl. Taste for seasoning and mix in the capers and vinegar. Leave to cool.

While the farro is cooking, lay the carrots in a roasting dish, drizzle on 2 tablespoons of the oil and half the thyme, then season with salt and pepper and add 2 tablespoons of water. Roast until they're cooked, about 30 minutes; you should be able to easily insert a sharp knife through them. Cut each into five or six pieces on an angle.

Lay the tomato halves, cut side up, on a baking sheet lined with baking parchment (to make it easier to clean). Mix the oregano, rosemary and the remaining thyme and 2 tablespoons of oil and drizzle this on the tomatoes. Sprinkle with a little salt and freshly ground black pepper. Bake for 40–50 minutes until the tomatoes have shrunk a little and coloured slightly.

To serve, toss the rocket (arugula) loosely through the farro and divide among your plates. Sit the carrots and tomatoes on top, pour on any roasting juices from either and then scatter with the Parmesan shavings.

Veggie Cheesy

CHAPTER 4

FOR 4 AS A STARTER OR 6 AS A SIDE DISH

Butternut squash with coconut, radicchio, endive and feta

WARM OR AT ROOM TEMPERATURE

INGREDIENTS

600g (1lb. 5oz.) butternut squash flesh, cut into large chunks

3 tbsp pumpkin seeds

½ tsp cumin seeds

2½ tbsp extra virgin olive oil

40g (1½oz/½ cup) desiccated (shredded) or 100g (3½oz.) fresh coconut, shredded (see recipe introduction)

½ head radicchio, cut lengthways

1 white endive (chicory; or you can use red)

125g (4½oz.) feta, crumbled (about scant 1 cup crumbled)

2 tbsp snipped chives

seeds from ¼ pomegranate

1 tbsp lemon juice

This is delicious on its own as a starter or as part of a larger meal. You could use pumpkin instead of butternut, or even celeriac or parsnips. I cracked open a whole coconut (see page 13), then used a vegetable peeler to peel strips off it but you can simply use any desiccated (shredded) coconut – short or long threads or strips. If feta isn't your thing, then replace it with coarsely grated (shredded) pecorino, manchego, aged Cheddar or Parmesan.

[METHOD]

Preheat the oven to 170°C (350°F/Gas mark 4).

Put the butternut in a roasting dish with the pumpkin seeds and cumin seeds, 1½ tablespoons of the olive oil and 1 tablespoon of water. Season with a little salt (not too much as feta is salty) and black pepper and mix together. Roast in the oven for 20 minutes, then stir in the coconut. Continue cooking, tossing every 10 minutes, until the butternut has coloured and you can insert a knife through it with little resistance. It should take about 30–45 minutes.

Separate the leaves of the radicchio, discarding the thick white stalks. Tear the larger outer ones up. Cut the base from the endive (chicory) and separate the leaves. Cut the larger leaves in half lengthways.

To serve, simply toss everything together with the remaining 1 tablespoon of olive oil, tasting for seasoning.

Roast pumpkin, steamed aubergine, shimeji and shiitake, herbed mascarpone and Parmesan

WARM

A salad for autumn (the fall), with lovely aromas coming from the lemon zest as it hits the warm vegetables. You can also add chestnuts to the vegetables while they're steaming, which adds great texture to the salad. Use the best quality Parmigiano Reggiano for this rather than some sad cheaper version. Alternatively, use something like Comté, an aged pecorino or manchego, or even a soft blue cheese.

INGREDIENTS

800g (1lb. 12oz.) pumpkin, peeled, deseeded and cut into large chunks

2 tsp cumin seeds

1 tbsp rosemary leaves

2 tbsp olive oil

1 aubergine (eggplant), cut into batons

200g (7oz.) shiitake mushrooms, stalks discarded, cut into wedges

200g (7oz.) shimeji mushrooms, caps separated from the bases

200g (7oz./scant 1 cup) mascarpone, at room temperature

2 tbsp shredded fresh soft herbs (basil, parsley, mint, coriander/cilantro, chervil)

1 spring onion (scallion), thinly sliced

2 handfuls salad leaves (I used mâche/corn salad but baby spinach, rocket/arugula or baby kale would work well)

30g (1oz.) Parmesan

1 juicy lemon

[METHOD]

Preheat the oven to 180°C (350°F/Gas mark 4).

In a roasting dish, mix the pumpkin, cumin, rosemary and 2 tablespoons of olive oil. Cover loosely with foil and bake for 20 minutes, then remove the foil and bake until golden, about another 25 minutes.

Meanwhile, steam the aubergine (eggplant) for 5 minutes. Add the shiitake and shimeji mushrooms to the steamer, gently tossing, and cook for an additional 4 minutes. It may be easier to cook them separately in a double-stack steamer, but bear in mind that the aubergine (eggplant) will take longer than the mushrooms.

Mix the mascarpone with the herbs, spring onion (scallion), ½ teaspoon of salt and a little black pepper.

To serve, lay salad leaves on your plates. Sit the pumpkin on and then the mushrooms. Dollop on the mascarpone, then shave the Parmesan and sprinkle on top. Grate the zest of half the lemon over the salad, then squeeze on the juice from the whole lemon.

FOR 6 AS A STARTER

Roast parsnips and celeriac, smoky apple compote, haloumi and pistachios

WARM OR AT ROOM TEMPERATURE

INGREDIENTS

400g (14oz.) haloumi, sliced 1cm (½in.) thick

2–3 (500g/1lb. 2oz.) eating apples

2 strips orange peel (with no pith)

1 tsp smoked paprika

60g (5 tbsp/⅓ cup) sugar

2 cloves, roughly bashed

2 tbsp cider vinegar

600g (1lb. 5oz.) parsnips, peeled, halved and sliced lengthways

1 large celeriac (600g/ 1lb. 5oz.), peeled, halved and sliced 5mm (¼in.) thick

1 leek, sliced into 1cm (½in.) rings

1 tbsp chopped mixed fresh hard herbs (rosemary, thyme, oregano, sage)

2 tsp coriander seeds, crushed

4 tbsp olive oil

2 handfuls salad leaves (I used baby kale)

50g (1¾oz./½ cup) toasted and roughly chopped pistachios

1 tbsp extra virgin olive oil

3 tbsp lemon juice

This combination of apple compote, chewy haloumi and sweet roast vegetables is terrific. It is a fairly rich salad but very delicious: it barely lasted until lunchtime when I cooked it for the photo shoot! This technique of soaking haloumi is a trick I learnt from Tarik and Savas in Istanbul and I've never looked back since. It turns a very firm and salty cheese into something more like firm mozzarella.

[METHOD]

Preheat the oven to 180°C (350°F/Gas mark 4).

Place the haloumi into a wide bowl or dish and pour on enough boiling water to cover by 3cm (1¼in.). Soak for 1 hour, then drain and pat dry on absorbent kitchen paper.

Peel and core the apples, then cut into chunks. Place in a pan with the orange peel, smoked paprika, sugar, cloves, vinegar and ½ teaspoon of salt. Bring to a simmer, then put a lid on and cook until softened, stirring from time to time. Once the apple is cooked, remove the lid and cook over a low heat to reduce the liquid by half. Turn off the heat and leave in a warm place with the lid on.

In a roasting dish, mix together the parsnips, celeriac, leek, herbs, coriander seeds and 2 tablespoons of the olive oil and season with salt and pepper. Roast until golden, about 40 minutes, tossing from time to time.

Place a frying pan (skillet) over a medium heat and add 1 tablespoon of olive oil. Fry half the haloumi until golden on both sides. Transfer to a warm plate and fry the other half in the remaining 1 tablespoon of olive oil.

To serve, toss the salad leaves with the roast vegetables and lay on a platter. Break the haloumi into pieces if the slices are large and sit on top of the vegetables. Spoon on the apple and cooking juices. Scatter with the pistachios, drizzle on the extra virgin olive oil and lemon juice and sprinkle with a little extra salt.

FOR 6 AS A STARTER OR SIDE DISH

Baby beetroot, broad beans, tarragon, goats' curd and hazelnuts

AT ROOM TEMPERATURE

INGREDIENTS

700g (1lb. 9oz.) mixed baby beetroot (beet), with leaves attached

85ml (⅓ cup) white vinegar

2 tbsp lemon juice

2 tsp English mustard

300g (10½oz.) podded broad (fava) beans (1.2kg/2lb. 10oz. unpodded weight)

4 tbsp tarragon leaves

1½ tbsp extra virgin olive oil

200g (7oz./scant 1 cup) goats' curd

50g (1¾oz./⅓ cup) hazelnuts, roasted, skins rubbed off, roughly crushed

This is a pretty and delicious salad to serve at home, at the beach or at a picnic. It can also be served topped with grilled (broiled) fish, roast lamb or cold roast chicken. If you can, source more than one colour of beetroot (beet): the final effect will be worth it. As you'll be boiling them, cook them in separate pans so the colours don't run. This amount of tarragon may seem excessive but young tarragon has such a refreshing anise flavour, you really can't use too much!

[METHOD]

Cut the leaves and stalks from the beetroot (beets) 1cm (½in.) above the beets. Discard any leaves that aren't looking their best and cut the remainder, leaves and stalks, into 4cm (1½in.) lengths. Rinse in cold water to remove any grit, then drain and set aside.

Wash the beetroot (beets) in tepid water to remove any dirt, then place in a saucepan with the vinegar and 2 teaspoons of fine salt. Add enough cold water to cover by 3cm (1¼in.) and bring to the boil. Reduce to a simmer and cook, uncovered, until you can insert a skewer through them, about 20–40 minutes depending on their size.

Leave to cool in the poaching liquid for 20 minutes, then drain and rub their skins off with your fingers or a small knife — wear gloves if using red beetroot (beets) to avoid staining your hands. Cut them in half lengthways if too large, and toss with the lemon juice and mustard.

While the beetroot (beets) are cooking, bring another pan of lightly salted water to the boil and cook the beetroot (beet) leaves for 90 seconds, then drain and refresh in a bowl of iced water. Drain again and squeeze out the excess liquid.

Boil the broad (fava) beans in salted water for 2–4 minutes depending on their size. Drain, refresh in cold water, then peel off their grey skins. Mix with the tarragon and olive oil.

To serve, mix the beetroot (beets) and their marinade with the leaves and lay them on a platter. Spoon on the broad (fava) beans and tarragon marinade. Dollop on the goats' curd, then scatter on the hazelnuts.

FOR 6 AS A STARTER

Goats' curd, golden beetroot, grapes, poached pear and ajo blanco

AT ROOM TEMPERATURE

INGREDIENTS

1 lemon, peeled, avoiding pith, and juiced

2 tbsp lemon juice

85g (3oz./scant ½ cup) caster (superfine) sugar

1 bay leaf

3 pears

½ medium-heat green chilli, thinly sliced into rings

250g (9oz.) golden beetroot (beet), peeled and sliced 5mm (¼in.) thick

300g (10½oz.) goats' curd (or use any other fresh white cheese)

100g (3½oz./1 cup) green and black grapes, thinly sliced

50g (1¾oz./⅔ cup) flaked almonds, lightly toasted

a little cress for garnish (I used red veined sorrel)

FOR THE AJO BLANCO

50g (1¾oz./⅓ cup) whole almonds, skinned (see above)

2 garlic cloves, sliced

30g (1oz.) slice sourdough bread, crusts removed, toasted then broken into pieces

2 tbsp sherry vinegar

4 tbsp olive oil

Ajo blanco is a chilled uncooked soup from Andalusia in Spain, which I've eaten and enjoyed many times, usually garnished with halved grapes. Here I use it as a very plentiful dressing. Choose cooking pears that are firm but ripe: varieties such as Comice, Anjou and Conference work well. Use whole almonds with the skin on and then remove the skin yourself for the best result. Simply place them in a heatproof bowl and pour on enough boiling water to cover by 3cm (1¼in.). Leave to cool, then peel the brown skin from them. Serve this in chilled soup plates with hot toasted crusty bread.

[METHOD]

First cook the pears. Place the peel and juice of the lemon and the extra juice in a medium pan with the sugar and bay leaf. Pour in water to 5cm (2in.) deep and bring to then boil, then reduce to a gentle boil. Peel the pears, cut them in half, remove the core and add to the poaching liquid. They need to be covered in liquid, so if they need a little more just add boiling water. Cover with a paper cartouche, or place a lid on the pan, and reduce the heat to a rapid simmer. Cook for 30 minutes, then leave to cool in the liquid for 10 minutes before removing with a slotted spoon. Once cooled, cut lengthways into slices 5mm (¼in.) thick.

Add the chilli to the liquid. Bring to the boil and reduce by half. Add the beetroot (beets) and cook until you can just insert a thin knife through them, about 10 minutes. Leave to cool in the liquid. Drain before using.

Make the ajo blanco. Place the almonds, garlic, bread and sherry vinegar in a blender with ¾ teaspoon of flaky salt and 200ml (¾ cup) of iced water and leave for 10 minutes. Purée on maximum speed for 20 seconds, then gradually drizzle in the olive oil while still blending. If it's very thick, add extra iced water. Taste for seasoning, adding more salt or sherry vinegar as needed. This will keep chilled in the fridge for a day. Store in a jar and shake well before using.

To serve, lay the beetroot (beets) on your plates and lay the pears on top. Add small pieces of goats' curd, then spoon the ajo blanco around it all and scatter with the grapes, flaked almonds and cress.

FOR 4 AS A MAIN COURSE OR 6 AS A STARTER

Baked ricotta and carrots, figs and smoky almond brittle

AT ROOM TEMPERATURE

INGREDIENTS

500g (1lb. 2oz./2 cups) ricotta

40g (1½oz./scant ¼ cup) grated Parmesan

½ tsp thyme leaves

¼ tsp chilli flakes

1 tsp nigella seeds

2 tbsp extra virgin olive oil

300g (10½oz.) small carrots, skins scrubbed

6 figs

1 handful salad leaves (I used baby kale, rocket/arugula and watercress)

6 kumquats, ends discarded, thinly sliced, pips discarded

1 lemon

85g (3oz.) smoky almond brittle (see page 124), broken into pieces

cress to garnish (I used red amaranth)

Baking ricotta transforms this relatively bland and crumbly cheese into something much firmer and very tasty when you spice it up – once you get the hang of it you can play around with spicing and flavours. The almond brittle (see page 124) is made even more delicious with the addition of smoked paprika. The recipe makes much more brittle than you need here – it's hard to make in smaller quantities – but I'm sure you'll use it up! The figs must be really ripe and plump for them to have a good influence on the salad.

[METHOD]

Preheat the oven to 175°C (350°F/Gas mark 4). Lightly brush a 20cm (8in.) square dish with ½ teaspoon of oil.

Crumble the ricotta into a bowl and mix with half the Parmesan, the thyme and ½ teaspoon of flaky salt. Press firmly into the prepared dish. Sprinkle with the chilli flakes, half the nigella seeds and the remaining Parmesan. Drizzle with 2 teaspoons of olive oil. Bake for 25 minutes, until golden, then take from the oven and leave to cool.

While the ricotta is cooking, bake the carrots. Place in a baking dish and toss with 1 teaspoon of olive oil, the remaining nigella seeds and some salt and pepper. Cook until you can easily insert a sharp knife through them, about 15 minutes depending on the size. Leave to cool.

Depending on the size and shape of your figs, either slice them into rounds or cut into wedges. I peeled mine as the skins were a little the worse for wear, but you can leave them unpeeled.

To serve, place the salad leaves on your plates and lay the carrots on top. Tuck in the figs and sliced kumquats. Break the ricotta into large chunks and place on top. Squeeze the lemon over the salad and drizzle with the remaining olive oil, scatter on the cress and tuck in pieces of the brittle.

Smoky almond brittle

INGREDIENTS

85g (3oz./1 cup) lightly
toasted flaked almonds

½ tsp smoked paprika

150g (5½oz./¾ cup) caster
(superfine) sugar

[METHOD]

Lay a piece of baking parchment on your work surface. In a bowl, mix the flaked almonds with the smoked paprika and ¼ teaspoon of flaky salt.

Place the sugar in a clean, dry, medium saucepan and melt over a medium heat without stirring. You can shake the pan gently to ensure it melts and colours evenly, but don't stir because if the sugar crystallizes, you'll have to start again. Once the sugar has become a dark caramel colour, turn off the heat and add the almonds. Stir to coat the nuts with caramel, then tip onto the baking parchment.

Lay another sheet of baking parchment on top, then roll it out as thin as you can while it is still hot. Leave to cool, then store in an airtight container.

Grilled carrots, manchego, orange, agave, pecans and sultanas

WARM OR AT ROOM TEMPERATURE

INGREDIENTS

600g (1lb. 5oz.) carrots, peeled, halved lengthways

3 tbsp olive oil

2 oranges, segmented

3 tbsp agave syrup (or use maple syrup)

50g (1¾oz./⅓ cup) sultanas (golden raisins, I used lovely green ones from Turkey)

100g (3½oz./1 cup) pecans, toasted and chopped

1 spring onion (scallion), thinly sliced

1 handful salad leaves (I used rocket/arugula)

60g (2¼oz.) manchego

This relatively simple salad will seem all the more fabulous if you use a few different colours of carrots. I found the combination of just two colours worked well and decided against using purple ones. I've also made this using baby carrots, which also looks and works a treat. Manchego is a fantastic ewes' milk cheese from La Mancha, near Madrid in Spain. If you prefer, you can use British Wigmore or Berkswell, Italian pecorino, or some other firm ewes' milk cheese – something you can shave or slice over the top. Agave syrup is a fabulous earthy sweet syrup, which complements the pecans – replace it with maple syrup if you can't find it, although most health food stores seem to carry it.

[METHOD]

Steam or boil the carrots in salted water for 6 minutes. If using baby carrots, cook for 4 minutes. Tip into a colander and leave to drain. Brush with 1 tablespoon of the oil and season with salt and pepper, then cook in a heavy-based pan until coloured on both sides and cooked through, about 3–4 minutes depending on their size. Leave to cool.

Mix the orange segments with any of their juice you can squeeze from the 'core'. Add the agave syrup, sultanas (golden raisins) and pecans. Leave for 10 minutes, then mix in the remaining oil. Leave for at least 20 minutes to allow the sultanas (golden raisins) to soak up some of the liquid, tossing from time to time. Just before serving, mix in the spring onion (scallion).

To serve, lay the carrots on a platter or plates. Scatter on the salad leaves, then spoon on the orange, sultana and pecan mixture. Thinly shave the manchego on just as you serve it.

FOR 6 AS A STARTER

Blue cheese, walnuts, grapes, cranberries, pear and argan oil

WARM OR AT ROOM TEMPERATURE

INGREDIENTS

3 pears, halved, core removed, and each half cut into six wedges lengthways

150g (5½oz./1½ cups) seedless grapes

50g (1¾oz./⅓ cup) dried cranberries (or use dried blueberries, currants or seedless sultanas/golden raisins)

75ml (5 tbsp) fresh orange juice

1 tbsp pomegranate molasses

1 tbsp olive oil

2 endive (chicory), leaves separated, larger ones sliced lengthways (I used red ones but green ones also look good)

4 leaves white radicchio, torn

6 frisée (curly endive) leaves (or use watercress, rocket/arugula or mâche/corn salad), torn

1 tbsp argan oil

100g (3½oz.) blue cheese, broken into chunks

85g (3oz./¾ cup) walnuts, toasted and roughly broken up

It's hardly original, making a salad with blue cheese, pear, walnuts and endive (chicory), but this is a delicious play on that classic French combination. Here, the pears are first roasted with grapes, dried cranberries, orange juice and pomegranate molasses, which makes it all taste so much better! Use firm but ripe cooking pears, and there's no need to peel them. I find this quite rich so prefer to serve it as a starter, but you might enjoy it as a main course. Argan oil is one of the culinary world's greatest ingredients. Harvested by women in Morocco, it's truly a marvel and well worth looking for – although it's expensive – but if you can't find it, you can use hazelnut or walnut oil instead. I used French Roquefort in my salad, but English Stilton, Spanish Cabrales or Italian Gorgonzola would work equally well.

[METHOD]

Preheat the oven to 170°C (350°F/Gas mark 4).

In a non-reactive roasting dish, mix together the pears, grapes, cranberries, orange juice and pomegranate molasses to coat everything evenly. Sprinkle on ½ teaspoon of salt and the olive oil. Cover loosely with baking parchment and bake in the oven for 15 minutes. Remove the paper and cook, stirring from time to time, until most of the liquid has evaporated, about 20 minutes. Leave to cool for 10 minutes.

In a large bowl, toss together all the salad leaves with the argan oil.

To serve, mix the leaves with the pears and pan juices and divide among your plates or platter. Scatter with the blue cheese and then the walnuts.

FOR 4 AS A STARTER

Crumbed camembert, apple, mango, salad leaves and radish

SALAD AT ROOM TEMPERATURE, CHEESE WARM

INGREDIENTS

oil for frying

1 ripe camembert (about 250g/9oz.), chilled, so it is firm enough to coat

50g (1¾oz./scant ½ cup) (all-purpose) flour

1 egg, beaten

100g (3½oz./1⅔ cups) breadcrumbs

1 mango, peeled and sliced

2 crisp eating apples, quartered and cored, then julienned

6 radishes, thinly sliced

1 tbsp runny honey

1½ tbsp lime juice

½ tsp finely grated lime zest

1 handful salad leaves (I used baby kale)

What could be better than deep-fried crumbed cheese? Yum yum! Whether you use goats' cheese, ricotta mixed with herbs and dried chilli and rolled into balls, mixed cheese scraps squashed together or, as here, camembert, deep-frying it in this way is like having grilled (broiled) cheese on toast! Culinary purists may feel that combining a classic French cheese with mango is too odd but my Italian burrata with mango dressing (see page 138) will prove that mango is a great accompaniment to cheese. This works much better as a starter than a main as the cheese is very rich.

[METHOD]

Heat 5cm (2in.) of oil in a medium pan to 180°C (350°F).

Cut the camembert into quarters. Toss in seasoned flour, coat with the beaten egg, then carefully coat with the breadcrumbs, making sure that the cheese is entirely coated. Return it to the fridge for at least 20 minutes to firm up.

Mix the mango, apples, radishes, honey, lime juice and lime zest together in a large bowl. As you toss it the honey will melt into the dressing. Add salt to taste.

As soon as you're ready, deep-fry the cheese wedges until golden on all sides and drain on absorbent kitchen paper. If the cheese begins to ooze out of the coating into the hot oil then carefully remove it, but not until it's golden.

To serve, place the salad leaves on four plates and spoon the mango salad on top. Place the deep-fried camembert wedges on top, cut in half to allow the hot cheese to ooze over the salad. Eat while hot.

Mozzarella, sherry-vinegar Medjool dates, popped cherry tomatoes and dukkah

AT ROOM TEMPERATURE

INGREDIENTS

1 large shallot, thinly sliced into rings

3 tbsp olive oil

2 tsp finely chopped or grated ginger

4 tbsp sherry vinegar

8 Medjool dates, quartered lengthways and pits removed

2 garlic cloves, thinly sliced

500g (1lb. 2oz.) cherry tomatoes

300g (10½oz.) mozzarella, at room temperature

3 tbsp picked soft herbs (basil, chervil, marjoram, fennel fronds)

2 handfuls salad leaves (I used watercress, baby kale and rocket/arugula)

4 tbsp dukkah (see page 134)

Marinating rich, filling Medjool dates in something sour like the sherry vinegar here, or even orange juice mixed with lime juice, softens their impact in a salad but also enhances it. Paired with the mozzarella (I used gorgeous fresh buffalo mozzarella) it's a dream combo. Dukkah (also spelt duqqa) is an Egyptian hazelnut-based condiment that New Zealanders have been using for more than a decade as a dip for bread doused in olive oil. It's worth making the quantity on page 134 and storing it in an airtight jar: although it's much more than you need for this recipe, you'll soon use it up. I've used almonds and pine nuts in my dukkah, but you can use pretty much any toasted nut.

[METHOD]

Sauté the shallot in 1 tablespoon of the oil over a medium heat until caramelized, about 5 minutes, stirring often. Add the ginger and sherry vinegar and bring to the boil. Remove from the heat and stir in the dates. Cover the pan and leave to macerate for at least 1 hour, stirring twice.

Heat the remaining oil in a large frying pan (skillet) over a medium heat. Add the garlic and let it sizzle briefly. Add the cherry tomatoes and cook, stirring gently, until they start to pop and some are beginning to split. Turn off the heat and leave to cool in the pan.

Cut or break the mozzarella into large chunks and gently toss with the herbs.

To serve, lay the salad leaves on a platter or plates. Lay the mozzarella on, then spoon on the tomatoes and their cooking juices and the dates and their liquid. Lastly, sprinkle on the dukkah.

Almond pine nut dukkah

INGREDIENTS

1 tbsp coriander seeds

1 tsp fennel seeds

1 tsp cumin seeds

2 tbsp sesame seeds (black or white, or a mixture of both)

¼ tsp sweet smoked paprika

100g (3½oz./⅔ cup) toasted almonds

50g (1¾oz./scant ⅓ cup) toasted pine nuts

[METHOD]

Place a heavy-based pan over a medium—low heat. Add the coriander, fennel, cumin and sesame seeds and cook until they become aromatic, shaking the pan as they do. Be careful not to colour too darkly: they will catch quite quickly and if you do burn them you'll need to start again! Once they're done, tip onto a plate and leave to cool.

Using a mortar and pestle, pound the toasted seeds with the smoked paprika. Add the almonds, pine nuts and 1 teaspoon of flaky salt and pound them coarsely. You might need to do this in two batches.

Store in an airtight jar for up to 2 weeks.

Grilled sweetcorn and asparagus with ricotta, goji berries and truffled honey dressing

WARM OR AT ROOM TEMPERATURE

This salad can be served either as a starter or a side dish. You could also turn it into a main by topping it with thinly sliced roast chicken, flaked smoked trout or salmon, shredded ham or sizzling bacon lardons straight from the pan. It's also great with ripe figs, peeled and sliced. Truffle oil is something that divides opinion – because most of the time it's just an aromatized oil that contains absolutely no actual truffle. I like it though – I find the slightly bitter taste, reminiscent of truffles, quite delicious – when used sparingly. You can also find fabulous truffle honey and use that in place of both the honey and truffle oil in this recipe. But, again some of these honeys contain no natural truffle at all. Alternatively, skip the truffle completely and substitute with argan oil, chilli oil, porcini oil or even a lovely aromatic lemon or orange oil. Goji berries (also known as wolf berries) are both colourful and tasty (they're slightly sour), and supposedly good for you. You can use them dried, but I like to soak and cook them briefly before using.

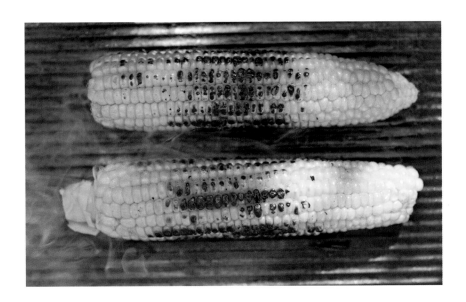

INGREDIENTS

2 corn cobs, husks peeled off

1½ tsp extra virgin olive oil

800g (1lb. 12oz.) asparagus, ends snapped off and discarded (about 450g/1lb. trimmed weight), lower part of the stalk peeled

2 tbsp goji berries

2 handfuls salad leaves (I used mâche/corn salad)

250g (9oz./1 cup) ricotta

2 tbsp sunflower seeds, lightly toasted in a dry pan or in the oven

1 orange

FOR THE TRUFFLED HONEY DRESSING

1½ tbsp extra virgin olive oil

1½ tsp truffle oil

2 tsp runny honey

2 tbsp lemon juice

1 tsp soy sauce (or use ½ tsp flaky salt)

[METHOD]

First grill the corn and asparagus. Put a heavy-based pan on a medium–high heat until smoking hot. Brush the cobs with ½ teaspoon of the olive oil and cook them, turning them as they become golden brown. Once they're coloured all over, or near enough, remove from the pan and leave to cool on a plate.

When cool enough to handle, cut into slices 1cm (½in.) thick. This might seem daunting but it's really not: lay a chopping board on your work surface on a damp tea (dish) towel (to prevent it sliding). Place the cobs, one at a time, on the board, and use a large knife to cut them. Trying to cut it with the tip end will be impossible, so sit the heel of the knife against the corn and press firmly down to cut through the core of the cob.

Toss the asparagus with 1 teaspoon of olive oil and cook in the pan until coloured, turning the spears as they cook. A finger-thickness spear will take about 90 seconds to cook over a high heat. Once done, remove from the pan and leave to cool.

Place the goji berries in a small pan, add enough water to just cover them and bring to a simmer. Cook until the water evaporates (this rehydrates them), then leave to cool.

Put all the dressing ingredients into a jar with a tight-fitting lid and shake vigorously. Taste for seasoning and add more soy or lemon juice if necessary.

To serve, put the salad leaves on a platter. Sit the asparagus and corn on top. Break up the ricotta with your fingers and scatter it on. Sprinkle on the sunflower seeds and goji berries. Shake the dressing again and drizzle it over. Using a fine grater, grate ½ teaspoon of zest from the orange directly onto the salad and squeeze the juice from half of the orange over the salad.

Burrata and tomatoes with mango dressing

AT ROOM TEMPERATURE

INGREDIENTS

600g (1lb. 5oz.) tomatoes

1 burrata (250–300g/ 10½–12oz.)

1 spring onion (scallion), thinly sliced and rinsed, then drained

FOR THE MANGO DRESSING

1 perfectly ripe mango (about 250–300g/9–10½oz.), peeled and all flesh cut from the stone (pit)

15 basil leaves

½ garlic clove, sliced

2 tsp finely chopped ginger

¼ medium-heat green chilli, chopped (including seeds)

¼ tsp finely grated lemon zest

2 tbsp lemon juice

3 tbsp vegetable oil

This was one of the stand-out dishes of the day during our first photo-shoot for this book. The burrata was as fresh as could be, recently arrived from Puglia in Italy; the mango was an Alphonso from India – ripe and aromatic; the tomatoes were perfectly coloured and full of summer-sunshine flavour. All I had to do was create a dressing that would bring harmony to the plate. Make sure you use a very ripe mango and avoid hothouse tomatoes: summer-sweet heirloom varieties look and taste best for this.

[METHOD]

To make the mango dressing, place all the ingredients except the oil into a jug and purée until smooth using a stick blender. Slowly add the oil and purée for 20 seconds. Add salt to taste. Alternatively, make in a jug blender; although, as this volume is quite small, you may have less success.

Thinly slice the tomatoes and arrange on a platter. Grind over some black pepper and sprinkle with flaky salt.

If your burrata has a solid 'knob' on it, then cut this off and thinly slice it. Break the burrata into chunks. Arrange the burrata slices and chunks on the tomatoes.

Drizzle with the dressing, sprinkle with the sliced spring onion (scallion) and serve immediately.

FOR 6 AS A STARTER

Grilled courgettes and broccolini, runner beans, cranberries and bocconcini

AT ROOM TEMPERATURE

INGREDIENTS

30g (1oz./¼ cup) dried cranberries

½ tsp fresh thyme leaves

2 tbsp lemon juice

3 tbsp olive oil

4 courgettes (zucchini), ends removed, sliced lengthways 5mm (¼in.) thick

250g (9oz.) broccolini, blanched for 30 seconds only, then refreshed and drained

300g (10½oz.) runner (pole) beans, topped and tailed, sliced on an angle, blanched for 3 minutes, then refreshed

6 radicchio leaves, shredded

12 bocconcini (300–400g/ 10½–14oz.)

This salad is lovely placed on the table alongside more simple salads as part of a hand-around family dinner. If you can't find bocconcini (very small mozzarella) then simply cut larger mozzarella into wedges or tear it apart into chunks. You can use dried cherries, dried blueberries or sultanas (golden raisins) in place of the dried cranberries if you prefer.

[METHOD]

Place the cranberries in a small pan with the thyme, lemon juice and 1 tablespoon of the olive oil and bring to the boil, stirring as it warms up. Simmer for 5 minutes, then take off the heat and leave to macerate for at least 30 minutes.

Meanwhile, toss the courgettes (zucchini) with the broccolini and remaining olive oil, season with salt and pepper and cook in a heavy-based frying pan (skillet), or place under a grill (broiler), to colour all over, about 2 minutes. Leave to cool.

To serve, mix the grilled (broiled) vegetables with the beans and radicchio and divide among your plates. Sit the bocconcini on the vegetables and spoon the cranberries and their marinade on top.

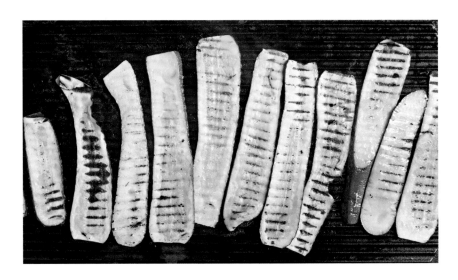

Miso-baked aubergine, dates, feta, crispy buckwheat and tahini yogurt

WARM OR AT ROOM TEMPERATURE

INGREDIENTS

3 tbsp miso paste (I used shiromiso)

3 tbsp mirin (or use 2 tbsp unrefined sugar + 1 tbsp water mixed together, or 2 tbsp runny honey)

2 tbsp sunflower oil (or light olive oil)

2 tbsp sesame oil

2 aubergines (eggplant), stems trimmed, each cut lengthways into six wedges

1 tbsp sesame seeds

2 tbsp tahini paste

3 tbsp orange juice

85ml (⅓ cup) Greek-style plain yogurt

½ tsp finely grated orange zest

2 tbsp extra virgin olive oil

2 handfuls salad leaves (I used baby kale and watercress)

10 Medjool dates (175g/6oz.), quartered lengthways and stone (pit) removed

200g (7oz.) feta, crumbled

2 tbsp crispy buckwheat (see page 156)

2 tbsp toasted pine nuts (or pumpkin seeds)

The Japanese rely on miso for the taste sensation of umami it adds to dishes, and I have been cooking with this fermented salty and sweet paste for almost 40 years and find it indispensible in my pantry. The one I use most often is a pale golden type called shiromiso (white miso – although it's generally not white at all), which is made from rice, barley and soya beans. Some types of miso – and there are hundreds – contain wheat, so if you are gluten intolerant, read the label. If you can't get Medjool dates (which are gorgeously toffee-like and plump), then use dried dates, which you'll need to slice and soak in warm water for 5 minutes to plump up before draining.

[METHOD]

Preheat the oven to 180°C (350°F/Gas mark 4).

Mix the miso paste with the mirin to loosen it, then stir in the sunflower and sesame oils. Brush the mixture thinly on the cut sides of the aubergine (eggplant). Sprinkle on the sesame seeds. Place on a baking sheet and bake for 20–30 minutes. The aubergine (eggplant) is cooked when you can squeeze it with little resistance.

Mix the tahini to a slurry with the orange juice. Stir in the yogurt, orange zest and 1 tablespoon of the olive oil, then season with salt.

Toss the salad leaves with the remaining 1 tablespoon of olive oil and divide among your plates. Sit the aubergine (eggplant) on top, then scatter with the dates, feta and crispy buckwheat. Finally, drizzle over the tahini yogurt, or serve it separately, and sprinkle with the crispy buckwheat and toasted pine nuts.

Mozzarella, artichokes, walnut sauce and sumac lavosh

AT ROOM TEMPERATURE

INGREDIENTS

½ lemon, sliced 1cm (½in.) thick

1 tbsp cider vinegar (or other white vinegar)

1 banana shallot, sliced into rings

½ carrot, peeled and sliced

1 bay leaf

1 tbsp fresh hard herbs (e.g. thyme, rosemary, oregano, sage)

1 garlic clove, sliced

125ml (½ cup) olive oil

8–10 (1kg/2lb. 4oz.) long-stemmed globe artichokes

1 handful salad leaves (I used pea shoots)

300g (10½oz.) mozzarella, torn into pieces

sumac lavosh (see page 146), as much as you like

FOR THE WALNUT SAUCE

50g (1¾oz./½ cup) walnut halves, toasted

40g (1½ oz.) slice sourdough bread (crusts left on), toasted then broken into pieces

75ml (5 tbsp) lemon juice

½ tsp finely grated lemon zest

2 garlic cloves, sliced

3½ tbsp olive oil

This cooking technique for the artichokes is termed 'à la grecque'. I like to use the smaller pointed variety of artichoke for this – but you can use the larger globe-shaped ones if that's what you have. Lavosh is a flatbread originating in the Middle East. It's easy to make and you can personalize it by adding your favourite seeds and spices – here I sprinkle it with sumac. The recipe on page 146 makes more than you need here as it's hard to make a small quantity. If you don't have time to make it, then serve with crostini or store-bought lavosh instead. The thick walnut sauce is similar to a Turkish tarator sauce, but interestingly it's made in a similar way to the Spanish ajo blanco on page 120.

[METHOD]

First cook the artichokes. Place the sliced lemon in a large saucepan with the cider vinegar, shallot, carrot, bay leaf, herbs and 1 garlic clove. Add the olive oil, 400ml (1⅔ cups) of water, ½ teaspoon of coarsely ground black pepper and 1½ teaspoons of salt. Cut the stalks off the artichokes 6–8cm (2½–3in.) from the base. Remove the lower leaves until you can feel them becoming more tender – this usually means removing the outer two or three layers, using either your fingers or a small knife. Using a small sharp knife, peel the tough skin from the stalks, working from the cut end towards the head, as the stalks are edible and I hate to waste good food! Cut through the heads crossways half-way up and discard the top part. Trim any hard pieces from the head itself. Cut in half lengthways. Carefully cut out the very fine 'choke' hairs, or use a small teaspoon to do this, but don't cut out any of the choke itself. As each artichoke is ready, add it to the saucepan and stir to coat in the oil and vinegar to prevent it from discolouring. Once all the artichokes are prepared, add just enough water to come to the top of the artichokes. Lay a paper cartouche on top, pressing it down, and poke a few holes in the paper. Bring to the boil, then reduce the heat to a gentle boil and cook until you can easily insert a thick knife through the base and stem of the artichokes, about 12–15 minutes. Leave to cool in the cooking liquid. They can be prepared up to 4 days in advance.

Make the walnut sauce. Place the walnuts, bread pieces, lemon juice and zest, 2 garlic cloves, 100ml (scant ½ cup) of iced water and ½ teaspoon of salt in a

[RECIPE CONTINUES]

[RECIPE CONTINUED]

small food processor (or use a stick or jug blender) and blitz to a purée. Add the oil and blitz again. Taste for seasoning.

To serve, lay the salad leaves on your plates and top with the mozzarella then the artichokes. Add some of the carrots, lemon slices and shallots from the cooking liquor, then dollop the walnut sauce on top. Finally, tuck in the sumac lavosh, broken into large shards.

Sumac lavosh

INGREDIENTS

170g (6oz./1⅓ cup) plain (all-purpose) flour, sieved

1 rounded tbsp wholewheat flour

1 tsp sugar

1 tbsp + 1 tsp extra virgin olive oil, plus extra or brushing

2 tsp sumac

[METHOD]

Preheat the oven to 180°C (350°F/Gas mark 4). Place the flours, sugar and ½ teaspoon of fine salt in a kitchen mixer (a stand mixer rather than a food processor) and mix together. With the motor running, add the oil and 85ml (⅓ cup) of iced water and mix together until a pliable dough is formed. If it's too dry, add a little extra iced water; if too wet, add a little extra wholewheat flour. Mix for 4 minutes on medium–low speed. Take the dough out, roll it on the work surface into a ball, then wrap in cling film (plastic wrap) and leave to rest for 30 minutes in the fridge.

Pull off walnut-sized pieces and roll out on a floured work surface as thin as you can. (At my restaurants we run it through our pasta rollers on the second thinnest setting.) Lay it on a baking sheet and leave to rest for 20 minutes (this will prevent it shrinking too much when baked). Bake until golden, turning the tray about 180° after 8 minutes to colour it evenly. The lavosh is ready when it has turned dark golden, about 15 minutes.

Remove from the oven and brush with oil and sprinkle with the sumac and some flaky salt while still hot. Once cooled, store in an airtight container. The dough freezes well and will last for 4 weeks, so just roll out what you need at the time.

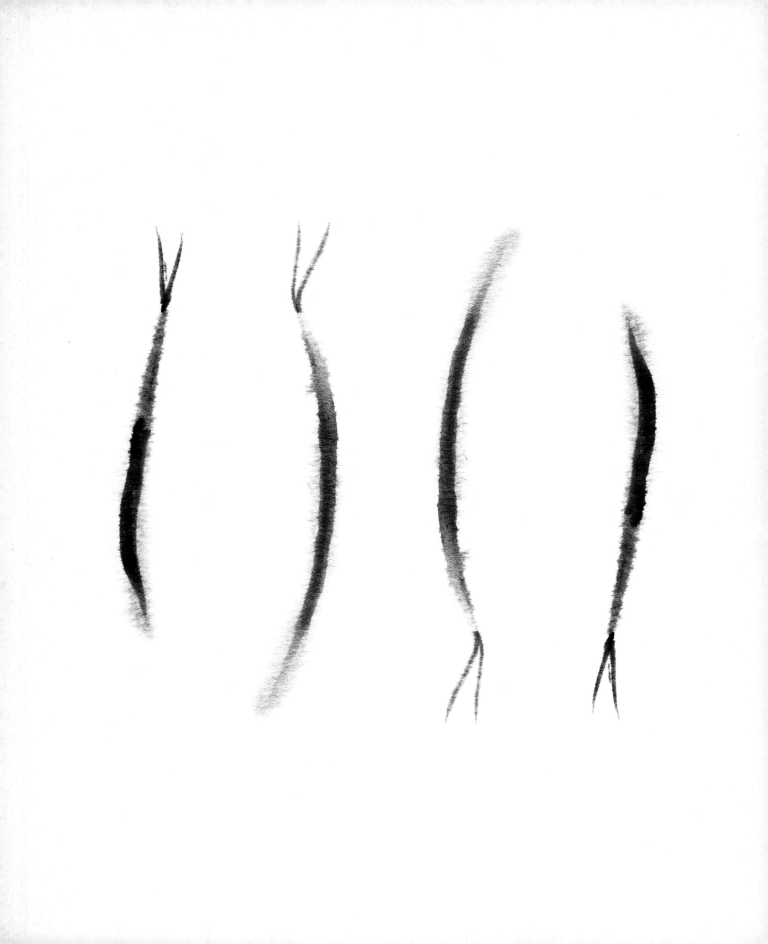

Fish and Shellfish

CHAPTER 5

Salmon sashimi, cucumber, tomato, ginger, almond and yogurt

SLIGHTLY CHILLED

INGREDIENTS

1 cucumber, peeled, halved lengthways and deseeded

16 cherry tomatoes, halved

3 tbsp lemon juice

2 tsp finely chopped or grated ginger

1 tsp wasabi paste (or use creamed horseradish or mustard paste)

4 tbsp Greek-style plain yogurt

4 tbsp soy sauce

4 tbsp mirin (or use 2 tbsp runny honey dissolved in 2 tbsp warm water)

700g (1lb. 9oz.) very fresh salmon loin (the thickest part), skin and bones removed

1 small handful salad leaves (I used wild rocket/arugula)

2 tsp extra virgin olive oil

20g (¾oz./¼ cup) flaked almonds, toasted

cress or micro-greens, for garnish (I used baby red-veined sorrel)

Rather like a generous sashimi assembly, this refreshing dish works a treat after a bowl of miso soup or tomato gazpacho. It can be made from most fish, but the oiliness of salmon works especially well with the cucumber. Other fish worth trying are halibut, bream (larger ones), tuna and cod, as well as scallops.

[METHOD]

Slice the cucumber 5mm (¼in.) thick crossways. Mix with the tomato halves, lemon juice, three quarters of the ginger and ½ teaspoon of salt. Leave to macerate for 30 minutes in the fridge. Drain before using.

Mix the wasabi into the yogurt and place in the fridge.

Mix the soy and mirin with the remaining ginger.

Slice the salmon 5mm (¼in.) thick and, when you're almost ready to serve, gently toss it with the soy mixture. Leave to marinate for 5 minutes, then drain in a colander, being careful not to crush the flesh.

To serve, lay the salad leaves and salmon on chilled plates. Scatter on the cucumber and tomatoes. Dollop on the yogurt, drizzle with the olive oil and sprinkle on the almonds, cress and some flaky salt.

Seared salmon, nori sauce, crispy buckwheat, gomasio and avocado

AT ROOM TEMPERATURE

INGREDIENTS

600g (1lb. 5oz.) chilled salmon loin (see recipe introduction), cut into four 150g (5½oz.) portions

light cooking oil

2 avocados

2 tbsp lime (or lemon) juice

¼ tsp finely grated lime (or lemon) zest

2 carrots, peeled, topped and tailed, then peeled into ribbons

100g (3½oz.) picked and washed watercress tips

4 tbsp nori sauce (see page 156)

4 tbsp crispy buckwheat (see page 156)

FOR THE GOMASIO

1 tbsp toasted white sesame seeds

½ tsp flaky salt

Everything except the searing of the fish can be done at least a few days ahead, so with good planning you'll be able to pull off what would seem to be a restaurant-quality dish. To really make this look fabulous you'll need to use the loin of the salmon, which is the thickest part of the salmon fillet. Make sure all skin and bones, and the blood line, are removed before you start. This is also delicious made with tuna. Goma is the Japanese word for sesame, and shio is the word for salt (or tide, as in a tidal sea), and gomasio (sometimes spelled gomashio) is a Japanese seasoning that I always have to hand: by pounding toasted sesame seeds with flaky sea salt you get a most delicious savoury seasoning that has much less salt, which has got to be good for you.

[METHOD]

Have a large bowl of iced water ready. Take the salmon from the fridge, pat dry with absorbent kitchen paper, then brush each piece with ½ teaspoon of oil and lightly sprinkle with salt.

Heat a heavy-based, ideally non-stick, frying pan (skillet). When it's smoking, place a portion of salmon in and cook for 15 seconds, then carefully, but quickly, roll it over to sear and colour all of the outer parts. Remove the salmon and plunge it into the iced water to prevent it cooking any further. Cook the remaining portions in the same way.

Once all four pieces have been submerged for 4 minutes, carefully remove from the water and pat dry on a tea (dish) towel. Place, covered, in the fridge for up to 6 hours before assembling.

Make the gomasio by roughly pounding the sesame seeds using a mortar and pestle, then pounding in the salt briefly, keeping it a little chunky.

Just before serving, remove the flesh from the avocados and cut into chunks. Toss with the lime juice and zest. Add the carrot and gently toss together with a quarter of the gomasio.

To serve, divide the salad among your plates and scatter with the watercress. Slice the salmon 5mm (¼in.) thick and lay this on top. Spoon the nori sauce on, then sprinkle with the remaining gomasio and the crispy buckwheat.

Nori sauce

INGREDIENTS

30g (1oz.) nori (about 10 sushi-sized sheets)

100ml (scant ½ cup) mirin

100ml (scant ½ cup) sake

75ml (5 tbsp) tamari (wheat-free soy sauce)

3 tbsp red wine vinegar

This makes much more than you need, but it is tricky to make a much smaller batch and it will keep in the fridge for 3 weeks if tightly covered.

[METHOD]

Carefully toast half of the nori over an open flame, in a frying pan (skillet) or under a grill (broiler). Because it's almost like paper it can catch fire, so keep an eye on it. You want it to change colour from almost black to green. Tear (or cut with scissors) both the toasted and untoasted nori sheets into very small pieces.

Put all the liquids in a pan and bring to the boil, then reduce to a rolling simmer and gradually stir in the nori until you have a thick pasty-looking mixture. Cook for 1 minute, stirring constantly.

Blitz with a stick blender to a paste, then chill and store in the fridge.

Crispy buckwheat

INGREDIENTS

50g (1¾oz./generous ¼ cup) whole buckwheat grains, rinsed and drained

about 300ml (1¼ cups) sunflower or other plain oil

You can make this up to a week in advance and store it in an airtight container. The quantities given here will make more crispy buckwheat than you need for this dish, but once you've tasted how good it is, you'll be sprinkling it onto everything from a simple green salad to a beef stew. Whole buckwheat should be easy to find at a health food store but as an alternative you could use toasted nuts or pumpkin seeds to give crunch to the dish.

[METHOD]

Pour 500ml (2 cups) of hot (but not boiling) water over the buckwheat in a bowl and leave for 6 hours or overnight.

Drain into a sieve, then pat dry on a kitchen cloth.

Pour enough oil into a medium pan or frying pan (skillet), about 24cm (10in.) diameter, to give you 2cm (¾in.) depth. Place over a medium heat and when the oil reaches 150°C (300°F), add the drained buckwheat.

Fry gently, stirring frequently, until the grains begin to stop sizzling and have turned golden brown. Drain in a heatproof sieve or small-holed colander, then lay it on baking paper, sprinkle with flaky salt and leave to cool. Once the oil has cooled you can strain and reuse it.

Beetroot-cured salmon, grilled artichokes, shredded cabbage, crème fraîche and pomegranate

I was in my local London Fields fishmongers when several fabulous wild Scottish salmon arrived. They weren't big, like farmed salmon, but they were really firm and I knew I wanted a whole fillet for this. If your salmon is larger and fatter, then it may need up to 72 hours curing. This style of curing with salt, sugar and lemon juice can also be applied to other fish fillets such as halibut, tuna or cod, as well as beef or farmed venison fillet. Ideally, cure it for 2 days before you need it so it has time to firm up once the marinade is wiped off. If you don't have time to cure the salmon, then use sliced cold-smoked salmon instead.

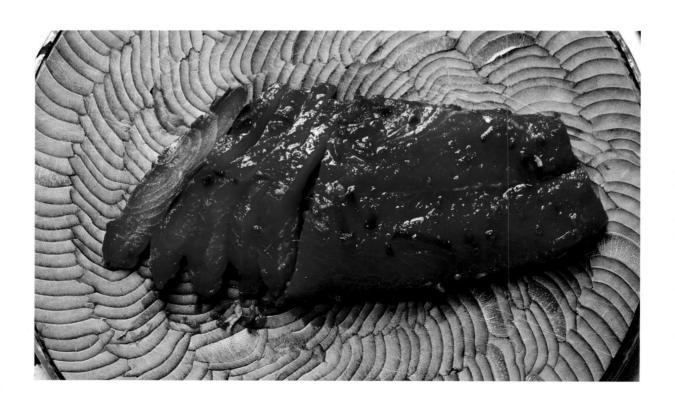

INGREDIENTS

2 tsp coriander seeds

½ tsp chilli flakes (or use ¼ fresh chilli or more to taste)

1 tbsp finely grated lemon zest

125g (4½oz./⅔ cup) golden or pale unrefined sugar

125g (4½oz./⅔ cup) coarse sea salt

4 tbsp grated ginger

1 red beetroot (beet) (raw or cooked), peeled and coarsely grated (shredded)

500g (1lb. 2oz.) salmon fillet, skin, bones and bloodline removed

3 tbsp lemon juice

2 juicy lemons

2 bay leaves

10cm (4in.) fresh thyme sprig

5cm (2in.) rosemary sprig

4 globe artichokes

2 tbsp extra virgin olive oil

300g (10½oz.) young Savoy cabbage, outer leaves and core discarded

2 tbsp grain mustard

1 tbsp finely snipped chives

200ml (¾ cup + 2 tsp) crème fraîche (thick sour cream)

3 tbsp pomegranate seeds

[METHOD]

Roughly pound the coriander seeds with the chilli flakes and half the lemon zest using a mortar and pestle. Mix in the sugar, salt and two thirds of the ginger. Wearing gloves, mix in the beetroot (beet). Tip a quarter of this curing mixture on the bottom of a non-reactive dish just large enough to hold the salmon and lay the salmon on top. Pile the rest of the cure on top, rubbing it evenly all over, and press down firmly. Drizzle on 1 tablespoon of the lemon juice. Press cling film (plastic wrap) down on the fish and seal tightly. Place in the fridge for 48 hours.

Wearing gloves, remove the salmon from the curing mix and wipe off any excess mixture. Pat the salmon with absorbent kitchen paper, then wrap it tightly in cling film (plastic wrap) and leave in the fridge for up to 4 days.

Bring a large saucepan of salted water to the boil. Slice one of the lemons 5mm (¼in.) thick and add to the pan along with the bay leaves, thyme and rosemary. Reduce the heat to a simmer and put a lid on.

Holding an artichoke by its stalk, pull the thick leaves from the base of the head until they begin to visibly thin and soften. Lay it horizontally on a chopping board and, using a sharp serrated knife, cut off and discard the top half. (Be careful as the head can slide around a little and they can be a little tough.) Cut the stalk off, near the base of the head, then trim off any rough edges using a small sharp knife. Using a teaspoon or a melon-baller, dig into the cavity of the artichoke to remove the hairy fibres. Cut the remaining lemon in half and rub each cleaned choke with them to prevent discolouring. Once all the artichokes are done, add to the pan of simmering water, making sure they're covered, and bring back to a gentle boil. Cook until you can insert a thin sharp knife through the thickest part (about 15 minutes depending on the size of the artichokes). Remove with a slotted spoon to a colander to drain and cool. Discard the poaching liquid.

Heat up a frying pan (skillet) or griddle pan. Slice the artichokes vertically 1cm (½in.) thick and toss with 1 tablespoon of the olive oil, salt and pepper. Grill until marked and coloured and leave to cool.

Shred the cabbage as thinly as you can. Mix the remaining ginger with the remaining 2 tablespoons of lemon juice, the mustard and a little salt and pepper. Mix this into the cabbage and leave in the fridge for at least an hour.

In a small bowl, mix the remaining lemon zest and the chives into the crème fraîche (thick sour cream).

To serve, unwrap the salmon and slice into 5mm (¼in.) thick pieces. Lay the cabbage on your plates, then the artichokes on top. Top with the salmon. Spoon on the crème fraîche (thick sour cream), drizzle with the remaining olive oil and scatter with the pomegranate seeds.

Poached salmon, almond and grapefruit couscous

WARM OR AT ROOM TEMPERATURE

INGREDIENTS

100g (3½oz./generous ½ cup) couscous

1 carrot, peeled and coarsely grated (shredded)

1 tbsp extra virgin olive oil

2 spring onions (scallions)

1 small handful flat-leaf (Italian) parsley on the stalk

1 grapefruit

2 salmon fillets (150–175g/ 5½–6oz. each), bones removed but skin left on

3 tbsp flaked almonds, lightly toasted and roughly chopped

1 small handful salad leaves (I used pea shoots)

1 lemon, halved

This is a healthy and light meal and you can serve the salmon straight from the poaching liquor or at room temperature. Poach the salmon in a saucepan wide and deep enough to hold the pieces in one layer. Ideally, it should be at least 8cm (3in.) deep. The couscous can also be served with a variety of other fish or meats, or topped with grilled (broiled) vegetables, salad leaves and toasted mixed seeds and nuts. Never use boiling water to soak your couscous – it makes it clump together.

[METHOD]

Mix the couscous with 100ml (scant ½ cup) of tepid water and ¼ teaspoon of salt and leave for 5 minutes. Mix in the grated (shredded) carrot and olive oil and leave for an additional 5 minutes. Trim both ends from the spring onions (scallions). Thinly slice the green parts and mix into the couscous. Pick the parsley leaves from their stalks (keep the stalks), coarsely shred and add to the couscous.

Put the parsley stalks and spring onion (scallion) white ends in a pan. Add water to a depth of 4cm (1½in.) and 1 teaspoon of salt, bring to the boil then reduce to a rapid simmer. Peel three strips of rind from the grapefruit, avoiding any white pith, and add to this poaching stock as it heats up.

Gently lower the salmon pieces into the simmering stock, skin side facing down, and bring back to the boil.

Turn off the heat, put a lid on the pan and leave for 8–10 minutes, by which time it will be cooked (if the salmon is thin, and submerged, then leave it for no more than 4–5 minutes).

Meanwhile, segment the grapefruit (see page 102). Cut each segment into three or four pieces and mix into the couscous along with the almonds and any juice you can squeeze from the grapefruit core.

To serve, divide the couscous among your plates and sit the pea shoots on top. Remove the salmon carefully from the poaching liquid and lay on a plate, skin side facing up. Peel off the skin and scrape away any dark-coloured flesh (the blood line) under the skin using a teaspoon. Break the salmon into flakes and sit it on top of the couscous. Tuck in a lemon half.

Hot-smoked salmon, avocado, pear, radish and horseradish cream

WARM OR AT ROOM TEMPERATURE

INGREDIENTS

600g (1lb. 5oz.) hot-smoked salmon fillet, skin, bones and bloodline removed, at room temperature

1 tsp extra virgin olive oil

100g (3½oz.) radishes

2 avocados

1 juicy lime (or small lemon)

2 tbsp creamed horseradish

3 tbsp crème fraîche (thick sour cream)

1 sweet, ripe pear

2 handfuls salad leaves (I used mâche/corn salad)

Hot-smoking is a technique whereby the ingredient is both smoked and cooked. The more familiar 'Scottish' cold-smoked salmon is smoked over very low temperatures and has the appearance of being uncooked. This salad can also be made using cold-smoked salmon, which has a more subtle flavour and is generally quite thinly sliced, or indeed the beetroot-cured salmon on page 158–60, but oven-warm chunks of salmon broken over the salad, combined with avocado, pear and horseradish, works best of all. Oily fish, horseradish and avocado truly are a great combination.

[METHOD]

Preheat the oven to 150°C (300°F/Gas mark 2). Line a baking sheet with baking parchment.

Lay the salmon on the baking sheet. Brush with the oil and warm in the oven. You don't want to 'cook' it as it's already cooked; you're simply warming it up. A fillet 2cm (¾in.) thick will take about 10–12 minutes.

Meanwhile, place the radishes in iced water for 10 minutes. Drain and cut them in half if they're large or leave whole.

Remove the flesh from the avocados and place in a bowl. Finely grate ¼ teaspoon of zest from the lime, then juice it. Add the zest and juice to the avocado and mash together roughly with a fork. Season to taste with salt and pepper.

In another bowl, mix the horseradish into the crème fraîche (thick sour cream) with a pinch of salt.

Cut the pear in half lengthways and remove the core and stem, then thinly slice it.

To serve, lay the salad leaves on your platter or plates. Break the salmon into chunks and sit it on top. Dollop on the avocado. Lay the sliced pear and radishes on top, then drizzle with the crème fraîche (thick sour cream).

Smoked mackerel, beetroot, egg, apple and dill miso mustard dressing

AT ROOM TEMPERATURE

INGREDIENTS

2 medium beetroot (beets; any colour)

1 tbsp extra virgin olive oil

2 tbsp lemon juice

1 small Chioggia beet (striped beet), for garnish

400g (14oz./about 4 fillets) smoked mackerel fillet

1 apple (choose one that's crisp, sweet and juicy)

1 handful baby salad leaves (I used mâche/corn salad)

4 eggs, soft boiled and peeled

FOR THE DILL MISO MUSTARD DRESSING

2 tbsp lemon juice

½ tsp pale miso paste

1 tsp grain mustard

½ tsp English mustard

½ tsp caster (superfine) sugar

2 tsp chopped fresh dill

2 tbsp extra virgin olive oil

The slightly bitter hints that smoking gives to a piece of fish and a generally sweetish cure is a perfect combination in my view. You can use any smoked fish for this, or even the teriyaki-style mackerel on pages 168–71. You can roast the beets in advance to save time, but wear gloves to prevent them staining your hands if you're using red or purple ones. There are many different styles of miso paste but generally the pale ones, such as shiromiso (white miso), will be sweeter, whereas darker ones, such as hatchomiso, will be more savoury. Taste the dressing to make sure it has a good combination of sweet and savoury.

[METHOD]

Preheat the oven to 180°C (350°F/Gas mark 4).

Wash any dirt off the two medium beetroot (beets), then wrap them up together tightly in foil. Place in a roasting dish and bake in the middle of the oven until you can insert a thin sharp knife or skewer through the foil into the centre of the beetroot (beets). This will take anywhere from 45 to 90 minutes depending on their size. Remove from the oven and leave until cool enough to handle. Still wearing gloves, unwrap from the foil and then use your fingers, and a small knife if needed, to rub and peel the skins from them.

Thickly slice the roast beetroot (beets) while still warm and toss with the olive oil, 2 tablespoons of the lemon juice and salt and pepper, then leave to cool.

Peel the Chioggia beet and slice as thin as possible into rings – a mandolin is ideal for this – and put in iced water to crisp it up.

Make the dressing. Mix the lemon juice into the miso paste to form a slurry. Mix in both mustards and sugar. Finally stir in the dill and the olive oil.

Remove the skin, bones and blood line from the mackerel, then break into chunks.

To serve, scatter the salad leaves on four plates. Lay the roast beetroot (beet) slices on top, then the mackerel and Chioggia beets. Cut the eggs in half and julienne the apple, discarding the core, and sit these on top. Spoon over the dressing.

Chilli-chocolate teriyaki mackerel with samphire, Jersey Royals and orange

WARM OR AT ROOM TEMPERATURE

The Japanese technique of teriyaki cooking is something well worth exploring. This sauce, which is sweet (from the mirin, sake or sugar) and salty (from the soy sauce), can be used to brush on or marinate fish, meat or vegetables, and becomes both savoury and sticky when brought into contact with high heat. In 2015, we held a collaborative dinner at The Providores with British chocolate guru Paul A. Young and he created a teriyaki glaze that contained chocolate, which we used on a beef dish. I was inspired, and this recipe takes a bow to Paul. Jersey Royals are very special potatoes grown on the slopes of Jersey's hillsides. They're fertilized with seaweed mulch and they're available for only a short period. If you can't source them, then use any small waxy potato. Samphire is a marsh vegetable that used to be very seasonal and was often hard to come by but is now farmed and more easily sourced. This way of multi-blanching then marinating it in lemon juice and olive oil is Turkish in style. You can replace it with very fine asparagus, beans or watercress if you wish. Although the samphire may lose some of its vibrant colour, the flavour is brilliant. If mackerel isn't your thing, then replace it with salmon fillet, tuna, or cod.

INGREDIENTS

2 large mackerel, filleted and small bones removed

500g (1lb. 2oz.) Jersey Royal or other small waxy potatoes

100g (3½oz.) samphire

2 tbsp extra virgin olive oil

1 tbsp lemon juice

2 oranges

1 handful salad leaves (I used rocket/arugula, but watercress would also be lovely)

FOR THE CHILLI-CHOCOLATE TERIYAKI SAUCE

2 tbsp soy sauce

2 tbsp mirin (or use 2 tbsp water and 1 tbsp caster/superfine sugar)

1 tsp runny honey

1 tsp finely chopped or grated ginger

½ tsp chilli sauce (Tabasco or a similar fiery sauce)

1 tbsp chopped or grated dark chocolate (60–75% cocoa solids)

[METHOD]

Lay the mackerel fillets in a shallow oiled baking dish, skin side down, then cover and place in the fridge.

Make the chilli-chocolate teriyaki sauce. Place the soy, mirin, honey, ginger and chilli sauce in a small pan and slowly bring almost to the boil, but don't boil it. Take off the heat and leave to cool for 1 minute, then stir in the chocolate until melted and emulsified. Pour into a clean bowl.

Scrub the skins of the potatoes and boil in lightly salted water until cooked, then drain. If they're small, serve them whole; if they're larger, cut them in half.

Pick any thick stems from the samphire and discard any discoloured parts. Place in a medium pan and cover with 5cm (2in.) of cold water. Bring to the boil and then drain in a colander. Cook again the same way twice more. Once drained for the third time, place in a bowl and stir in the olive oil and lemon juice. Add the potatoes and mix together.

Cut the peel and pith from the oranges, then slice them 5mm (¼in.) thick, discarding any pips.

Preheat a grill (broiler) to its highest setting. Remove the fish from the fridge and brush half the teriyaki sauce over the flesh side. Cook under the grill (broiler) until it begins to caramelize. Remove from the heat and carefully turn over the fillets. Brush the skin with the remaining sauce and cook until bubbling and golden.

To serve, lay the orange slices on your plates. Mix the salad leaves with the potatoes and samphire and lay them on top. Carefully lift the mackerel fillets out of the baking dish and sit them on top.

FOR 2 AS A MAIN COURSE OR 4 AS A STARTER

Tuna with coconut, chilli, mango, apple and lime

SLIGHTLY CHILLED

INGREDIENTS

350g (12oz.) very fresh tuna loin, skin and bones removed

3 tbsp lime juice (or use lemon juice)

1 small red onion, halved and very thinly sliced

½ tsp finely grated lime zest

½ medium-heat red chilli, finely chopped (use more or less to taste)

1 tsp grated palm sugar or light brown sugar

1 ripe, sweet mango

100ml (scant ½ cup) coconut milk

8 stalks coriander (cilantro), leaves picked

1 spring onion (scallion), thinly sliced

1 crisp, sweet apple

2 tbsp desiccated (shredded) coconut, toasted

Raw fish salads have been part of my family's culinary repertoire back in New Zealand for as long as I can remember. Even my step-mum, Rose, a Cockney from London's East End, got into the swing of things when she and Dad married. Whether it be a Peruvian ceviche or Cook Island's Ika Mata, or even a jumble of Japanese sashimi, raw fish is delish! Pretty much any fish, so long as it's very fresh, will work here. The smaller the chunks of fish, or the thinner it's sliced, the less time it'll take to marinate. If your limes are very firm, you can get the most juice from them by rolling them firmly on their sides along your worktop for 10 seconds, which helps to crush the cell walls inside the flesh. Alternatively, as odd as this may seem, zap them for 15 seconds in the microwave and then leave to cool.

[METHOD]

Cut the fish into cubes about 1½–2cm (¾in.) square. Mix with half the lime juice and ¼ teaspoon of flaky salt, then cover and leave in the fridge for 30 minutes.

Briefly rinse the sliced onion under cold water, then mix with the lime zest, chilli, palm sugar and remaining lime juice. Cover and place in the fridge until the fish is ready.

Peel the skin from one half of the mango and cut off the cheek (you'll need only one cheek). Thinly slice the flesh.

Drain the juices from the fish. Toss gently with the onion mixture, coconut milk, mango, coriander (cilantro) and spring onion (scallion). Cover and leave for 5 minutes in the fridge.

Cut the apple (unpeeled) into juliennes and toss with the toasted coconut.

To serve, give the fish another gentle mix and taste for seasoning, adding extra salt if needed. Divide among your bowls or plates and sprinkle the apple and coconut on top.

Herb-roast cod and cauliflower, courgettes, broad beans, watercress and pomegranate

WARM OR AT ROOM TEMPERATURE

INGREDIENTS

1 medium cauliflower, green leaves and excess stalk removed

2 tbsp mixed fresh herbs, chopped (e.g. thyme, oregano, mint, rosemary, tarragon, parsley)

4 tbsp olive oil

600g (1lb. 5oz.) cod fillet, bones and skin removed

1 tbsp pomegranate molasses

2 tbsp lemon juice

2 courgettes (zucchini), topped and tailed, sliced lengthways 5mm (¼in.) thick

125g (4½oz.) broad (fava) beans, blanched and refreshed, peeled if large

1 large handful watercress, washed and picked, thick stalks discarded

2 tbsp pomegranate seeds

Fish and cauliflower, both roasted, are a great combination of flavours and textures, especially if the cauliflower is slightly crunchy. There are many varieties of cauliflower, with several colours – in this recipe I used a lovely purple one. I also used yellow courgettes (zucchini) instead of the usual green ones for their colour. As you're not cooking them, make sure they are firm and fresh. The key to success with this dish is to slightly undercook the fish – it will finish cooking as it rests.

[METHOD]

Preheat the oven to 200°C (400°/Gas mark 6).

Separate the cauliflower florets and place in a roasting dish. Add half the herbs, 1 tablespoon of olive oil, salt and pepper and toss together. Cook in the top of the oven until coloured, about 15–20 minutes.

Brush a roasting dish with 1 teaspoon of the oil and lay the fish in it. Season with salt and pepper, sprinkle with the remaining herbs and drizzle with 2 teaspoons of olive oil. Bake until the fish is just cooked: fillet pieces that are 3cm (1¼in.) thick will take about 12 minutes. To test, poke a knife into the centre of one of the thicker pieces and gently prise apart. If it's translucent, it's perfect.

Make the dressing. Mix the pomegranate molasses, lemon juice and 1 tablespoon of olive oil together with ¼ teaspoon of salt. Taste and add more salt if needed.

Toss the sliced courgettes (zucchini) with the remaining 1 tablespoon of olive oil and lightly season with salt.

To serve, toss the cauliflower with the courgettes (zucchini) and broad (fava) beans. Scatter with the watercress. Gently break the fish up using a spoon and fork and place it on top. Drizzle with the dressing and scatter the pomegranate seeds over the top.

Grilled octopus with potato, bean, onion and dill salad

WARM OR AT ROOM TEMPERATURE

INGREDIENTS

1 large octopus (about 3kg/6½lb.)

2 red onions, thinly sliced into rings

75ml (5 tbsp) cider vinegar

2 tsp sugar

500g (1lb. 2oz.) waxy potatoes, unpeeled, skins scrubbed

extra virgin olive oil, for reheating the octopus and drizzling at the end

150g (5½oz.) beans, green and yellow, blanched and refreshed

3 tbsp snipped dill

2 lemons, each cut into quarters

Octopus may seem daunting to cook, but it's not really that hard and is well worth the effort. It's fine to use frozen octopus rather than fresh: in fact, some claim that it's even better because the freezing causes cell walls within the flesh to rupture, which tenderizes it. This technique of slowly baking the octopus, rather than boiling it, comes from Paul Melville, the talented chef running The Providores kitchen when we shot this dish. If you can't find a large octopus, then use two or three smaller ones instead and reduce the cooking time. You can eat the octopus at room temperature, but I like to serve it warmed up under the grill (broiler) or on the barbecue. This salad teams really well with the watermelon and feta salad on page 29.

[METHOD]

First cook the octopus. Preheat the oven to 140°C (275°F/Gas mark 1). Bring a large pan of water to the boil (large enough to hold the octopus easily — or cut it into two or more pieces if this helps) and add 1 teaspoon of fine salt per litre of water. Brush a cake rack with oil, and sit it inside a roasting dish of a slightly larger size, lined with baking parchment. Cut the head off the octopus from just above where the tentacles meet and remove the inner guts. Cut the mouth out of the octopus and remove the beak — these are both located where the tentacles meet. Carefully lower the tentacles and head into the water and boil for 1 minute. Using tongs, remove and lay on the oiled rack. Cover the octopus with baking parchment, tucking it into the dish, then cover this with foil, or an upturned baking dish that sits snugly and will keep the moisture in. Cook in the oven for 3½ hours. Check to see if the octopus is tender: its texture should still be firm, but you should be able to easily cut through a tentacle at the thickest part. Remove and allow to cool. Cut between the tentacles once cooled, and slice the head into strips.

While the octopus is cooking, toss the onions with 4 tablespoons of the cider vinegar, the sugar and ½ teaspoon of salt. Cover and leave to marinate in the fridge, stirring several times.

Boil the potatoes in lightly salted water until cooked, then drain and thickly slice as soon as they are cool enough to handle. Toss with the remaining 1 tablespoon of vinegar. Keep at room temperature.

[RECIPE CONTINUES]

[RECIPE CONTINUED]

Preheat a grill (broiler) to high. Lightly oil a baking sheet and lay the tentacles and sliced head on it, then brush them with a little extra oil. Place under the grill (broiler) and cook until the octopus skin begins to bubble and almost blister.

To serve, drain half the liquid from the onions, then toss them with the potatoes, sliced octopus head, beans and dill. Divide among your plates, lay an octopus tentacle on top along with any juices from the baking sheet. Drizzle with a little extra virgin olive oil and serve with the lemon wedges.

Grilled squid and peppers, freekeh, chillied aubergine and sesame peanut brittle

WARM OR AT ROOM TEMPERATURE

INGREDIENTS

1kg (2lb. 4oz.) uncleaned squid

2 garlic cloves, peeled and thinly sliced

2 (bell) peppers (red, orange or yellow), cut in half, stalk and seeds removed, then sliced into strips

3 tbsp olive oil

200g (7oz./1 cup) freekeh, rinsed and drained

1 handful flat-leaf (Italian) parsley leaves

2 spring onions (scallions), thinly sliced

2 juicy lemons

¼ tsp finely grated lemon zest (from one of the above lemons)

1 aubergine (eggplant), sliced into 1cm-thick rings

1 medium-heat red chilli, finely chopped

1 small handful coriander (cilantro), including stalks, shredded (or use parsley, fennel or dill fronds)

2 tbsp soy sauce

6 tbsp crushed sesame peanut brittle (see page 180)

This lovely flavoursome salad can be served hot off the grill or barbecue, or at room temperature, so it's the perfect meal to cook last minute at a barbecue, or at home, finished before your guests arrive to avoid all that smokiness filling the house. The perfect-sized squid tubes to use will be about 12–15cm (5–6in.) long, but you can make do with much smaller ones or even larger ones – just adjust your cooking times accordingly. The sesame peanut brittle is very easy to make and keeps for 2 weeks if stored in a cool place in an airtight container.

[METHOD]

First clean your squid. Separate the heads from the tentacles and remove the wings. Split the heads in half lengthways and using a knife, scrape out any of the inner workings of the heads. Remove the beaks from the centre of the legs. Peel off any membrane from the wings and head and place the cleaned squid and tentacles into a colander and leave to drain for a few minutes. Pat dry with absorbent kitchen paper and put in a dish. Add the garlic, sliced peppers and 1 tablespoon of olive oil and mix together, then cover the dish and leave for 30 minutes in the fridge.

Meanwhile, pour water into a medium pan until three quarters full and bring to the boil. Add the freekeh and 1 teaspoon of salt, and cook over a rapid simmer for 20 minutes or so until cooked. It should have a little bite to it still but not be crunchy. Drain into a sieve and leave to cool. Once cooled, mix with 1 tablespoon of olive oil, the parsley, spring onions (scallions), the juice of 1 lemon and the lemon zest. Taste for seasoning.

Cut the other lemon into four or six segments.

Brush the aubergine (eggplant) slices with the remaining 1 tablespoon of olive oil and season lightly. Cook on a griddle, or in a heavy-based frying pan (skillet) placed over a medium–high heat, until both sides are golden and marked, about 2 minutes on each side. Once cooked, put on a baking sheet and sprinkle with half the chopped chilli and coriander (cilantro). Turn over and sprinkle with the remainder and a little salt and pepper.

[RECIPE CONTINUES]

[RECIPE CONTINUED]

Turn the heat almost up to full, then cook the squid and peppers together (using the same pan or griddle you used to cook the aubergines/eggplant – there is no need to clean it), turning as the squid cooks and curls up. Cook in two batches so you don't overcrowd the pan or griddle, which will lower the temperature. Make sure you don't overcook the squid either, or it will become tough. Once the second lot of squid and peppers are almost cooked, pour in the soy sauce, return the first batch and cook until the soy sauce has evaporated, tossing everything. Turn off the heat and place the squid and peppers in a bowl.

To serve, layer the aubergine (eggplant) with the freekeh on a platter or plates. Pile on the squid and peppers. Scatter with the crushed sesame peanut brittle and tuck a lemon wedge in.

Sesame peanut brittle

INGREDIENTS

100g (3½oz./⅔ cup) roasted peanuts, salted or unsalted – just adjust the amount of salt you add

2 tbsp sesame seeds, toasted

150g (5½oz./¾ cup) caster (superfine) sugar

[METHOD]

Line a baking dish or heatproof tray with baking parchment.

Mix the peanuts, sesame seeds and ¼ teaspoon of flaky salt together.

Place the sugar in a clean, dry saucepan and melt over a medium heat without stirring. You can shake the pan gently to ensure it melts and colours evenly, but don't stir: if the sugar crystallizes, you'll have to start again.

Once the sugar has become a dark caramel colour, turn off the heat and add the peanut mixture all at once. Stir to coat the nuts with caramel, then tip onto the baking parchment, press as flat as you can and leave to cool. It will be really hot so do be careful.

You can either break this up with your fingers, carefully chop it with a sharp knife while still a little warm, or place it inside a strong plastic bag and bash with a rolling pin until crushed. Store the brittle in an airtight container.

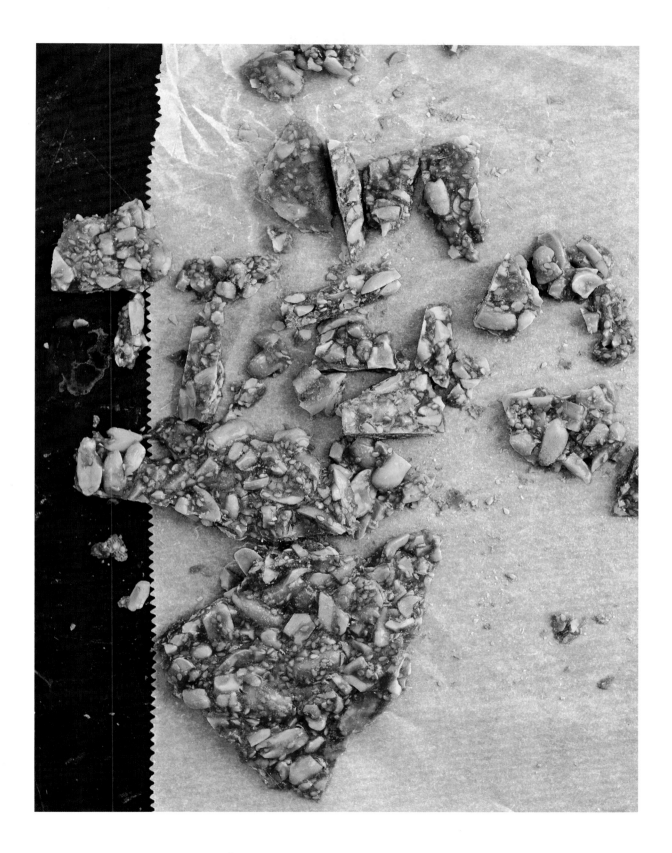

Grilled prawns, bacon and bananas, avocado and chilli mayonnaise

WARM

INGREDIENTS

250g (9oz.) raw peeled prawns (shrimp) (500g/ 1lb. 2oz. unpeeled weight)

1 ripe banana

2 tbsp vegetable oil

1 large shallot, thinly sliced into rings

¼ tsp finely grated lime zest

2 tsp lime juice

4 tbsp mayonnaise or egg-free milk aioli (see pages 264 and 266 respectively)

chilli sauce, to taste

4 rashers smoked streaky (pork belly) bacon

2 large slices bread for toasting (I used Turkish flat bread)

1 avocado

1 generous handful baby spinach or other salad leaves

Prawns (shrimp) and bacon make a great combination, especially if the bacon is smoked, slightly crisp when cooked and deliciously salty. Fresh, high-quality prawns (shrimp) are a little 'crunchy' in texture, rich and slightly sweet, and the two combined are terrific. Add grilled (broiled) banana (a childhood breakfast favourite of mine served with bacon) to the mix for the perfect casual brunch or supper pick-me-up! You can use either the mayonnaise or egg-free milk aioli (see pages 264 and 266 respectively) as the base for the chilli mayonnaise.

[METHOD]

Peel the prawns (shrimp) but keep the tails on. (You can freeze the shells for making a delicious bisque at some later point.) Run a small sharp knife along the 'spine' of the tail and remove and discard the digestive tract.

Peel the banana and slice on an angle 5mm (¼in.) thick. Gently toss or brush both the prawns (shrimp) and the banana with the oil.

Rinse the shallot rings in cold water for a minute, separating them, then drain. Mix with the lime zest and 1 teaspoon of the juice.

Mix the mayonnaise with the remaining 1 teaspoon of lime juice and the chilli sauce to taste. Check for seasoning, adding salt if needed.

You can cook this either under the grill (broiler), in a frying pan (skillet) or on a barbecue. Heat the grill (broiler) or pan (skillet) medium–high and cook the bacon until crisp and bubbling with fatty juices. Remove from the heat and keep warm nearby. Cook the prawns (shrimp) for no more than 60 seconds on each side, depending on their size. Sit the prawns (shrimp) with the bacon and keep warm. Cook the banana on both sides until beginning to caramelize. It'll be quite soft when you turn it over, so treat it gently. Remove from the heat.

Toast the bread. Peel the avocado, remove the stone (pit), scoop out the flesh and cut into wedges.

To serve, gently mix the prawns (shrimp), bacon, banana, shallots, avocado and spinach together, then pile on top of the toast. Serve with the chilli mayonnaise.

Salt and Sichuan pepper prawns, miso-roast Jerusalem artichokes, crispy garlic and umeboshi dressing

WARM

This can easily be scaled up to make it a starter for many people, or served as a main course for two alongside a crisp green salad. You need to use smallish raw prawns (shrimp); don't use cooked ones. Sichuan pepper is a tongue-numbing spice from China, also called Sansho pepper in Japan. It's an acquired taste and, though I love it, I have several friends who can't bear it. If you can't source it, then use black pepper instead. If Jerusalem artichokes aren't in season, use chunks of celeriac, sweet potato or pumpkin. Umeboshi are salted sour Japanese fruits called 'ume' (they're not plums as many people think, but more closely related to the apricot). You can buy them whole in jars, or as a paste. If you can't find them whole then use 2 teaspoons of paste.

INGREDIENTS

500g (1lb. 2oz.) Jerusalem artichokes, skins scrubbed (or peeled if really dirty)

1 tbsp miso paste (I used shiromiso)

1 tbsp olive oil

2 tsp sesame seeds

4 whole umeboshi, pitted and roughly chopped

1 large shallot, finely chopped

1 spring onion (scallion), thinly sliced

2 tsp finely chopped or grated ginger

1 tbsp sugar

½ tsp finely grated lime zest (or lemon zest)

75ml (5 tbsp) lime juice (or use lemon juice)

2 tsp fish sauce

1 tbsp Sichuan peppercorns

2 tbsp flaky salt

3 tbsp rice flour (or use cornflour/cornstarch, tapioca flour or even wheat flour)

vegetable oil for deep-frying

6 garlic cloves, thinly sliced

500g (1lb. 2oz.) peeled headless raw prawns (shrimp) – butterfly them by splitting them in two, but keeping them connected at the tail

1 handful coriander (cilantro), picked, stalks cut into 2cm (¾in.) lengths

1 large juicy lime, quartered

[METHOD]

Preheat the oven to 180°C (350°F/Gas mark 4). Line a roasting dish with baking parchment.

Slice the Jerusalem artichokes 5mm (¼in.) thick. Mix the miso with the olive oil, sesame seeds and 2 teaspoons of warm water. Toss with the artichokes, then place in the roasting dish and bake until golden, about 20 minutes. Stir from time to time so they become evenly coloured.

Make the dressing. Mix together the umeboshi, shallot, spring onion (scallion), ginger, sugar, lime zest and juice and fish sauce.

For the salt and pepper mixture, dry-toast the Sichuan peppercorns in a frying pan (skillet) over a medium–high heat for 1–2 minutes until fragrant, shaking the pan as they cook. Add the flaky salt and cook for an additional 20 seconds, gently shaking the pan the whole time. Tip into a mortar and pound until reasonably fine, but not powdered, with a pestle. Once cooled, mix into the rice flour in a bowl.

Pour oil into a wok or deep-sided pan to a depth of 1cm (½in.) and heat until it begins to smoke a little (at about 160°C/325°F).

Scatter the sliced garlic onto the surface of the oil as quickly as you can to enable even cooking, stirring the oil gently as the garlic becomes golden. If it turns dark brown it will likely taste bitter and burnt, but too pale and it won't become crispy. Once done, remove with a slotted spoon and drain on absorbent kitchen paper.

To fry the prawns (shrimp), top up the oil to a depth of about 5cm (2in.) and increase the temperature to 180°C (350°F). Pat the prawns (shrimp) dry with absorbent kitchen paper. Toss them in a bowl with the Sichuan pepper flour and leave for 30 seconds. Shake off the excess flour and place the prawns (shrimp) on a tray. Fry them in two or three batches until golden and crisp, then drain on absorbent kitchen paper. Don't overcrowd them in the pan or the oil temperature will drop and they will taste oily.

To serve, place the artichokes on your platter or plates. Scatter on the coriander (cilantro) stalks, then lay the prawns (shrimp) on top. Spoon on the dressing, scatter with the coriander (cilantro) leaves and crispy garlic and tuck in the lime quarters.

Clams, mussels, puy lentils, coconut, samphire, tomato and shiitake mushrooms

WARM

INGREDIENTS

100g (3½oz./½ cup) puy lentils

2 large shallots, finely chopped

4 garlic cloves, sliced

2 tbsp sesame oil

1kg (2lb. 4oz.) clams, rinsed well and cleaned, opened or damaged ones discarded

1kg (2lb. 4oz.) mussels, rinsed well, cleaned of beards, opened or damaged ones discarded

400ml (13½fl. oz.) can coconut milk (unsweetened)

4 tomatoes, halved, seeds squeezed out, diced

300g (10½oz.) shiitake mushrooms, thickly sliced, stalks discarded

100g (3½oz.) samphire, any woody stems discarded

The broth created when making this dish is so delicious, it's almost worth making it just for that, so make sure you serve it with some bread to mop up the delicious juices. You'll also need to serve your guests with finger bowls as they'll need to be hands-on to enjoy this.

[METHOD]

First cook the lentils. Rinse them in a sieve for 15 seconds, then put in a saucepan and cover with 5cm (2in.) of water. Add ½ teaspoon of salt. Bring to the boil then cook at a rapid simmer until done, which will take about 20 minutes. Drain.

Heat the sesame oil in a large pan on a medium heat and fry the shallots and garlic until caramelized. Add the shellfish and cook for 1 minute, gently stirring the whole time. Stir in the coconut milk and bring to the boil. Put a lid on and cook for 3 minutes. Give the pan a stir and then keep cooking only until the clams and mussels are open. Scoop them out into a colander, discarding any that haven't opened. Put the coconut broth back on a high heat and reduce by half. Add the tomatoes, shiitake mushrooms and samphire and boil for 1 minute.

Save a handful of the best-looking clams and mussels in their shells (I allowed six clams and four mussels per person). Remove the flesh from the remaining ones and discard the shells.

To serve, mix all the shellfish into the broth and taste for seasoning, adding salt and coarsely ground black pepper as needed. Ladle into warmed bowls.

Oysters, roast tomatoes, celery, dashi jelly and chillied sesame dressing

SLIGHTLY CHILLED

INGREDIENTS

6 plum tomatoes, halved lengthways

½ tsp finely chopped thyme

½ tsp finely chopped tarragon

¼ tsp dried chilli flakes

1 tbsp extra virgin olive oil

1 handful watercress, picked

12–16 oysters, freshly shucked

2 young celery stalks (from the centre of the bunch), thinly sliced

FOR THE DASHI JELLY

10–12g kombu seaweed (a 10cm x 12cm/4 x 5in. piece), briefly rinsed under warm water and wiped dry

3½ tbsp soy sauce

3½ tbsp mirin

10g (⅓oz.) dried shaved bonito

1 heaped tsp (4g) agar powder

FOR THE CHILLIED SESAME DRESSING

1 shallot, finely chopped

¼ medium-heat red chilli, finely chopped including the seeds (more or less to taste)

½ tsp finely grated lime zest

4 tbsp lime juice

I love this salad served icy cold, made with freshly shucked oysters. However, I've also served it in cooler months using oysters that I've poached briefly in a mixture of dashi and cream. To do that, make double the quantity of dashi given here and combine half of it with an equal amount of coconut milk or cream. To set the jelly, I use agar powder, which is a seaweed-based 'vegetarian gelatine', but you can replace it with regular gelatine. The dashi stock makes more jelly than you need but it's very hard to make any less. Make your jelly first, and keep it in the fridge for up to 5 days. You can also buy dashi granules from Japanese stores. Allow three or four oysters per person, depending on their size.

[METHOD]

Make the dashi jelly at least 3 hours before serving. Place the kombu, soy sauce, mirin and 400ml (1⅔ cups) of water into a pan and very slowly bring almost to the boil — make sure it doesn't actually boil though. Turn off the heat and add the bonito. Stir briefly, then let it settle for 15 minutes. Strain through a fine sieve into a clean pan — you should have 400ml (1⅔ cups) of liquid. Bring it to a rapid simmer, then remove from the heat and sprinkle the agar powder on the surface, gently whisking it in. Put the pan back on the heat and slowly bring it to a gentle boil, gently whisking the whole time, and cook for 1 minute. Pour into a heatproof dish and leave to set and cool. (Interestingly, agar jellies will set while still warm.) Cover and chill in the fridge for up to 5 days. Cut the jelly into long batons, thin strips or any other shape that takes your fancy.

Preheat the oven to 160°C (325°F/Gas mark 3). Line a roasting dish with baking parchment.

Place the tomato halves in the roasting dish, cut side facing up. Scatter evenly with the thyme, tarragon and chilli flakes. Drizzle on the olive oil and lightly season with salt. Bake for 45 minutes or so until they have coloured and slightly shrunk. Remove from the oven and leave to cool.

2 tbsp mirin (or use 1 tbsp caster/superfine sugar and 1 tbsp water)

1 tbsp sesame oil

2 tsp fish sauce (or use light soy sauce or ¼ tsp salt)

2 tbsp finely snipped chives

Make the chillied sesame dressing. Place the shallot, chilli, lime zest and juice, mirin, sesame oil and fish sauce in a jar and shake well. Leave in the fridge until you need it. Just before using, add the chives and shake again.

To serve, lay the watercress on your plates, sit the tomatoes on top and tuck in the oysters. Scatter over the celery and top with strips of dashi jelly. Spoon on the dressing.

Raw scallops, jicama, cucumber, radish, seaweed, passion fruit dressing and macadamia nuts

CHILLED

INGREDIENTS

300g (10½oz.) scallops, cleaned, coral (roe) removed and saved

2 tsp extra virgin olive oil

5g dried seaweed

¼ jicama (about 100g/3½oz.), peeled and julienned or shaved

2 small cucumbers (or use ½ a regular cucumber), peeled, deseeded and sliced lengthways

4 radishes, thinly sliced

1 spring onion (scallion), thinly sliced

50g (1¾oz./⅓ cup) macadamia nuts, lightly toasted and roughly chopped

FOR THE PASSIONFRUIT DRESSING

4 tbsp fresh passionfruit pulp (3 or 4 passion fruit depending on how plump they are)

2 tbsp lime juice

1 tbsp soy sauce

1 tsp finely chopped or grated ginger

½ green chilli, finely chopped with seeds (more or less to taste)

2 tsp chopped or grated palm sugar (or light brown sugar)

2 tbsp sunflower oil

You need to use the best scallops you can buy for this dish. If you're unable to source them then you can use the freshest raw fish, cooked prawns (shrimp) or even thinly sliced smoked salmon instead. The scallop coral (roe) adds a surprisingly delicious flavour element so don't discard them. Jicama is also known as yam-bean and should be available in Southeast Asian supermarkets. If you have trouble finding it, you can substitute it with kohlrabi or nashi pear. Dried seaweed is now fairly easy to source and there are myriad types, from sea spaghetti and sea salad through to varieties such as arame, dulce and nori, to name but a few. They're all quite different and will add colour, texture and innovation to your salad. If the seaweed you're using is thick, steam it for 10 minutes after soaking, then refresh it under cold water and drain. I like eating passionfruit seeds as I enjoy their crunch and colour, but you may prefer to strain them out.

[METHOD]

Depending on how thick your scallops are, cut them horizontally into two or three slices. Place in a non-reactive dish and sprinkle with ¼ teaspoon of salt and the olive oil. Cover and put in the fridge. Chop the coral (roe) into pieces and place in a small bowl in the fridge.

Soak the dried seaweed in boiling water for 30 minutes, then drain.

Make the passionfruit dressing. Place the passionfruit pulp, lime juice, soy sauce, ginger, chilli and palm sugar in a jar and shake vigorously until the sugar has dissolved. Add the sunflower oil and shake again.

Mix a third of the dressing into the coral (roe). Put back in the fridge for 10 minutes.

To serve, toss the jicama, cucumber, radishes, spring onion (scallion) and seaweed together and divide among four chilled plates. Lay the scallop slices on, then spoon on the coral (roe). Spoon on the remaining dressing and sprinkle with the macadamia nuts.

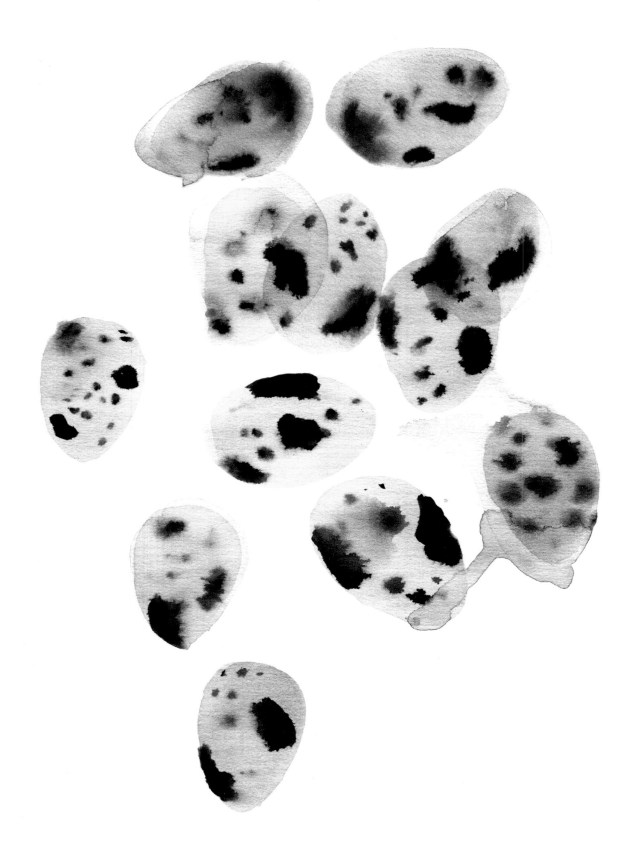

Poultry

CHAPTER 6

FOR 6 AS A MAIN COURSE

Roast chicken, kumquats, black garlic, kale and avocado

WARM OR AT ROOM TEMPERATURE

INGREDIENTS

8 boneless chicken thighs

8 black garlic cloves, sliced

8 kumquats, unpeeled, thinly sliced

2 tsp fresh rosemary (or fresh thyme or oregano or a mixture)

4 tbsp sunflower seeds

2 tbsp avocado oil

1 small red onion, thinly sliced into rings

200g (7oz.) kale, thick stem removed and discarded

2 avocados

2 tbsp lemon juice

1 cucumber, ends discarded, thinly sliced

Black garlic is a delicious fermented garlic that adds a lovely treacle–caramel flavour and depth to dishes without a strong raw-garlic after-taste. It is becoming easier to find, but if you have no luck, you can use regular garlic. Kumquats are great here, too, adding a slight bitterness because you use them unpeeled; if unavailable, substitute thinly sliced lemon, mandarins or oranges. Avocado oil works well in any dish that contains avocado. It has a high burning point, which means it is terrific for roasting and pan-frying. Olive oil or sunflower oil are fine to use instead if you can't get hold of it.

[METHOD]

Preheat the oven to 180°C (350°F/Gas mark 4).

Place the chicken thighs, garlic, kumquats, rosemary and sunflower seeds in a roasting dish. Pour on the avocado oil and 2 tablespoons of water and season with salt and pepper. Toss everything together. Roast, turning the chicken several times while cooking, until the chicken is cooked through and the skin is golden and crispy, about 30–40 minutes. Remove from the oven and leave until cool enough to handle, then cut each thigh into four or five slices.

While the chicken is cooking, soak the onion in cold water for 10 minutes, then drain.

Meanwhile, blanch or steam the kale for 3 minutes. Tip it into a colander and, when it is cool enough to handle, squeeze out as much water as you can, then coarsely shred it.

Remove the flesh from the avocados and cut into chunks. Mix with the lemon juice to prevent it going brown.

To serve, toss the kale, onion, cucumber and avocado together and lay it on the bottom of a serving dish. Lay the chicken on top then spoon over the contents of the roasting dish.

Coconut-poached chicken, prosciutto, melon, croutons and spinach

WARM OR AT ROOM TEMPERATURE

INGREDIENTS

400ml (13½fl. oz.) can coconut milk (unsweetened)

5cm (2in.) piece ginger, peeled and thinly sliced

3 kaffir lime leaves (or use ½ tsp finely grated lime zest)

2 tsp fish sauce (or use 1 tsp flaky salt)

½ medium-heat chilli, chopped, including seeds (more or less to taste)

4 chicken breasts (fillets), about 175g (6oz.) each, skin attached (it helps keep it juicy and you'll peel it off once cooked)

8 slices slightly stale bread, 5mm (¼in.) thick

1 tsp olive oil

200g (7oz.) baby spinach

1 tbsp lime juice (or use a little extra of lemon juice)

400g (14oz.) melon, seeds and skin removed, sliced into wedges or chunks

125g (4½oz.) thinly sliced prosciutto

Because this salad is very simple, you need to make sure every ingredient is perfect. Use a tasty free-range or organic chicken breast (fillet), and if you can find one that's been on an organic corn-fed diet, even better. Melons are truly good only when they're ripe and sweet. I used both galia and cantaloupe melon, but even watermelon would be good here. Either Italian prosciutto or Spanish jamón will work well. For the croutons, I bought some olive focaccia from the local deli. Baby spinach was looking particularly good the day we photographed this, but mâche (corn salad), baby gem or wild rocket (arugula) would also be delicious. Really, apart from assembling the ingredients, all you need do is poach the chicken in a coconut broth and this can be done from 3 hours to a day ahead. The poaching stock that's left over makes a delicious Thai-style chicken soup, but it's also great used as the stock for a spinach, pea and ginger risotto. So much deliciousness!

[METHOD]

Preheat the oven to 170°C (350°F/Gas mark 4).

Pour the coconut milk into a large saucepan, then rinse out the can out with the same volume of water and add to the pan. Add the ginger, lime leaves, fish sauce and chilli and bring to the boil. Put a lid on the pan and simmer for 10 minutes. Turn the heat back up, remove the lid and bring almost to the boil.

Place the chicken breasts (fillets) into the pan, skin side down, then reduce to a simmer and cook with the lid on for 8 minutes. Carefully turn them over using tongs and cook for an additional 3 minutes. Turn off the heat and leave to cool in the liquid for 20 minutes.

Meanwhile, make the croutons. Lay the sliced bread on a baking sheet and brush lightly with the oil. Bake until they begin to crisp up and turn pale golden. Turn over and bake on the other side for 5 minutes. Remove from the oven and cook on a cake rack.

Remove the chicken from the pan and place on a tray to cool. Strain the poaching liquid through a fine sieve into a jug and leave to cool. Just before serving, peel off the skin and slice the chicken breasts (fillets) at an angle about 7mm (¼in.) thick.

To serve, toss the baby spinach leaves with 4 tablespoons of the cooled coconut poaching liquid, the lime juice and a few pinches of salt. Arrange the leaves on your plates and sit the sliced melon on top. Lay the chicken pieces on and then the prosciutto. Tuck in the croutons.

Poached chicken, green tea noodles, grilled baby corn, daikon, pomegranate and lemongrass

AT ROOM TEMPERATURE

INGREDIENTS

1 chicken (about 2kg/4½lb.)

3 litres (13 cups) chicken stock (or water)

125ml (½ cup) soy sauce

10 star anise

2 x 6cm (2½in.) cinnamon sticks

1 tbsp coriander seeds

1 clementine (or mandarin or orange), sliced into six

4 black garlic cloves (or use smoked garlic or ordinary garlic), sliced

6 dried (or 12 fresh) shiitake mushrooms

100g (3½oz.) ginger, peeled and sliced

4 tbsp honey, agave syrup, palm sugar or demerara sugar

250g (9oz.) green tea noodles

2 tbsp sesame oil

500g (1lb. 2oz.) baby corn

2 tsp sunflower oil

3 spring onions (scallions), thinly sliced

300g (10½oz./2 cups) podded edamame beans, blanched

300g (10½oz.) daikon, peeled and thinly sliced into discs

seeds from ½ pomegranate

Poaching poultry (or other meats) in stock is nothing new, but in parts of China, this 'master stock' is used again and again, which makes it incredibly tasty and concentrated. Once you've cooked the chicken for this salad, strain the stock and use again, or freeze it as it is or reduce to a quarter of the volume and freeze. Either way, next time you use it, taste for seasoning before you poach your chicken and either add more aromatics or dilute it with more water. Green tea noodles (cha soba) are generally made with wheat and buckwheat flours but it's the powdered green tea that gives it a lovely colour and flavour. Buckwheat noodles, vermicelli or Chinese egg noodles also work well for this salad.

[METHOD]

Cut the legs/thighs from the chicken carcass, keeping them in one piece. Cut off the wings. If your chicken came with the neck, rinse this. Rinse the inside of the body cavity. In a pan large enough to hold all of the chicken pieces, add the chicken stock, soy sauce, star anise, cinnamon sticks, coriander seeds, clementine, sliced garlic, shiitake mushrooms, ginger and honey. Bring to the boil and simmer, covered, for 20 minutes. Add the wings and legs/thighs and bring back to the boil, then reduce to a simmer and cook for 10 minutes. Add the carcass and cover with boiling water, bring to the boil, then reduce to a simmer and cook, covered, for 12 minutes. Turn off the heat and leave the chicken in the stock for 5 hours without removing the lid.

Remove the legs, thighs, wings and carcass from the poaching stock. Remove the meat from the bones, cut into pieces, cover and set aside. Strain 200ml (¾ cup) of the stock into a clean jar for the dressing.

Make the dressing. Add the lemongrass, ginger and vinegar to the reserved stock and give the jar a good shake. Add salt to taste and leave at room temperature, or store in the fridge, for up to 1 hour. This dressing needs to be very punchy!

Drop the noodles into a large pan half-filled with lightly salted boiling water. Bring back to the boil, then stir in 200ml (¾ cup) of cold water. (This is known as 'shocking the noodles'.) Do this once more as soon as the water comes back to

FOR THE DRESSING

5cm (2in.) lemongrass stem from the lower end, two outer layers discarded, insides thinly sliced

1 tbsp grated or finely chopped ginger

2 tbsp balsamic vinegar (or use Chinese black vinegar)

reserved stock (see method)

the boil, then lower the heat to medium and cook until the noodles are al dente. Drain into a colander and rinse until cool under running water. Tip into a large bowl and toss with the sesame oil.

Toss the baby corn with the sunflower oil. Cook over a high heat in a frying pan (skillet) or griddle pan until coloured all over, then tip onto the noodles. Add the spring onions (scallions), half the edamame, half the daikon, half the pomegranate seeds and 2 tablespoons of the dressing, then divide among your plates.

Lay the chicken on top of the noodle salad, then scatter with the remaining edame, daikon and pomegranate seeds. Shake the dressing again and spoon over the chicken.

Chicken livers, quinoa, roast fennel, hazelnuts, mushroom purée and tarragon crème fraîche

WARM

INGREDIENTS

2 heads fennel, trimmed and thinly sliced lengthways

2 garlic cloves, thinly sliced

8 sage leaves, shredded

1 tbsp olive oil

100g (3½oz./generous ½ cup) quinoa, cooked and drained (see page 75)

60g (2¼oz./¼ cup) butter

1 tsp finely grated or chopped ginger

150g (5½oz.) open-cap mushrooms, thinly sliced

150g (5½oz./⅔ cup) crème fraîche (thick sour cream)

1 tbsp tarragon leaves

½ red onion (or 2 shallots), thinly sliced

500g (1lb. 2oz.) chicken livers, cleaned of sinews and veins

1 tbsp balsamic, sherry or red wine vinegar

60g (2¼oz./generous ⅓ cup) hazelnuts, toasted, skinned and coarsely chopped

One of the great classic salads is the combination of warm chicken livers and baby spinach tossed with croutons and mustard vinaigrette. This dish is inspired by that classic and I really enjoyed creating it. If you're not a fan of offal, think of this as a sort of warm pâté!

[METHOD]

Preheat the oven to 190°C (375°C/Gas mark 5).

Place the fennel, garlic, sage and olive oil in a roasting dish and toss together. Roast for 30 minutes or so, tossing as it cooks from time to time, until the fennel becomes golden. Once done, mix in the cooked quinoa and keep warm.

Melt a third of the butter in a saucepan over a medium heat and add the ginger. Cook for 30 seconds, gently stirring to prevent it catching. Stir in the mushrooms, 2 teaspoons of water and ½ teaspoon of flaky salt. Put a lid on the pan and cook until the mushrooms are cooked, stirring from time to time. Once they're done, remove the lid, stir in 100g (3½oz./scant 1 cup) of the crème fraîche (thick sour cream) and cook for an additional 2 minutes, stirring as it cooks. Purée smooth using a stick blender or small food processor, taste for seasoning and keep warm.

Pound the tarragon leaves with a pinch of salt using a mortar and pestle. Mix in the remaining crème fraîche (thick sour cream) and set aside.

Heat a frying pan (skillet) over a medium heat. Add another third of the butter and the onion and sauté until the onion caramelizes, stirring as it cooks. Remove to a small plate. Add the remaining butter and, when sizzling, add the chicken livers. Cook for 1 minute, then turn over and cook on the other side for 2 minutes. The livers will be pink at this stage; if you prefer them well done, then cook them for a bit longer. Return the onion to the pan and add the balsamic vinegar, hazelnuts and some salt and pepper. Mix into the livers and cook for 10 seconds.

To serve, divide the mushroom purée among four warmed plates, spreading it out with the back of a spoon. Lay the fennel and quinoa on next. Spoon on the livers and the pan juices, then dollop on the tarragon crème fraîche (thick sour cream).

Twice-cooked sweet-chilli quail with deep-fried egg and sweetcorn

WARM

INGREDIENTS

5cm (2in.) cinnamon stick

2 star anise

1 shallot, sliced

3 tbsp soy sauce

85g (3oz./scant ½ cup) grated palm (or demerara) sugar

1 medium-heat chilli, red or green, sliced, including the seeds (more or less to taste)

2 garlic cloves, sliced

4 tsp finely chopped or grated ginger

4 quails, boned and flattened out (spatchcocked)

1 corn cob, husks removed, cut in half (see page 136)

4 large eggs, at room temperature

150g (5½oz.) silken tofu

1 small bunch coriander (cilantro), shredded

2 tbsp lime juice

¼ tsp lime zest, finely grated

2 tsp sesame oil

vegetable oil for deep-frying

6 spring onions (scallions), trimmed and cut into 5cm (2in.) lengths

1 carrot, ends trimmed, peeled, then peeled into ribbons

1 small handful flat-leaf (Italian) parsley leaves

This really does work best with boned quails, and you can ask your butcher to bone them for you, but if that's not possible, then use whole un-boned quails; it'll just be a little more difficult to eat them. If your quail are small, serve one and a half per person. Deep-frying boiled eggs may seem a strange idea, but we've been serving them as a snack in The Providores for years, and there's something quite delicious and a little quirky about them – golden eggs on the outside that have runny inner yolks. The tofu dressing resembles mayonnaise when made, although it's much lighter, and it also goes well with steamed chicken breasts (fillets) and fish, or drizzled over barbecued pork chops.

[METHOD]

First poach your quail in a medium pan. Put the cinnamon stick, star anise, shallot, soy sauce, palm sugar, chilli, garlic and half the ginger in the pan. Add 700ml (3 cups) of water and bring to the boil, then turn the heat down to a simmer and cook for 15 minutes. Bring back to the boil and lower in two of the quail, skin side facing up, and cook for 1 minute. Reduce the heat to a rapid simmer, then turn them over and cook for an additional 2 minutes. Remove with tongs on to a plate and cook the other two in the same way. Leave to cool, then cut each one into four, cutting the legs and thighs from the body, then cutting through to separate the breasts (fillets). Lay on absorbent kitchen paper. Reserve the poaching liquor.

Once the quail are done, keep boiling the poaching liquor until it has reduced by two thirds, then strain into a heatproof bowl and keep warm.

Half-fill a medium pan with lightly salted water and bring to the boil. Add the corn and boil for 2 minutes, then remove and place in a bowl of iced water. After a minute, remove to a colander and drain. Cut the kernels from the cob using a sharp knife.

While the water is still boiling, carefully lower the eggs into it using a slotted spoon and boil for 4 minutes 15 seconds. A medium egg will be soft boiled at this stage; cook up to a minute more for large eggs, or if you don't like your yolk runny. Remove from the boiling water and place in iced water to cool. Drain after 10 minutes, then carefully peel, making sure you don't damage the egg white.

[RECIPE CONTINUES]

[RECIPE CONTINUED]

Place in a bowl of water until you need them. (Being supported in the water stops them collapsing.)

In a small food processor bowl, or using a stick blender, purée the remaining 2 teaspoons of ginger with the tofu, coriander (cilantro), lime juice and zest and sesame oil until green and smooth. Add ¼ teaspoon of flaky salt.

Pour oil into a wok or saucepan to a depth of about 6cm (2½in., deep enough to submerge an egg) and heat to 180°C (350°F). Deep-fry the spring onions (scallions) until collapsed and just beginning to colour, stirring gently as they fry, then drain on absorbent kitchen paper. Deep-fry the carrot ribbons until crispy, stirring gently the whole time to prevent them burning, then drain on kitchen paper. Make sure the parsley leaves are dry so that they don't splatter, then deep-fry until crisp, again stirring gently as they fry and draining on kitchen paper. Sprinkle everything with a little flaky salt.

Remove the eggs from the water and pat dry with kitchen paper. Gently lower the eggs into the hot oil and cook for about 5 minutes, until golden brown. Carefully stir them in the oil as they fry to ensure even cooking. Remove with a slotted spoon onto a plate – avoid using absorbent kitchen paper as it may stick to the eggs.

The quail will be easier to cook in two batches: deep-fry the legs together first, then the breasts (fillets). Lower the pieces carefully into the hot oil and deep-fry until golden and a little crisp, about 2 minutes, stirring gently as they cook. Remove from the fryer and place in the bowl of quail-poaching liquor, toss together and leave to marinate. Cook the breasts (fillets) next. Quail breasts (fillets) are best cooked pink, so even though they're thicker, deep-fry for just 90 seconds, gently stirring as they fry. Drain from the oil and toss with the marinating legs.

To serve, lay the spring onions (scallions), carrots and parsley on your plates and scatter over the corn kernels. Serve two legs and two breasts (fillets) per portion. Place an egg on each plate – which you can serve whole or broken up, then finish by spooning on the dressing.

Duck, figs, walnuts, grapes, sherry vinegar and membrillo

WARM

INGREDIENTS

2 duck breasts (fillets)
(125–175g/4½–6oz. each)

125g (4½oz.) membrillo, cut
into chunks

2 tbsp sherry vinegar

1 garlic clove, crushed

60g (2¼oz./½ cup) walnuts,
toasted

¼ tsp olive oil

4 figs, stalk removed, halved
lengthways

1 small handful salad leaves
(I used baby kale and pea
shoots)

100g (3½oz./1 cup) grapes,
halved

Make this in the autumn (fall) when the figs and grapes are sun ripened, rich and sweet. I used delicious black grapes that tasted of port and small black figs from Turkey, which are packed with flavour and spectacular when cooked. Membrillo is a firm quince 'paste' or 'cheese' from Spain. (You can, of course, make it, but that's not a recipe for this book.) The thick purée made from it here makes more than you need, but it's hard to make less and it will keep in the fridge for 2 weeks.

[METHOD]

Score the skin of the duck breasts (fillets) in a cross-hatch pattern, cutting through the skin, but not down into the flesh. Remove the sinews from the flesh side of the breasts (fillets). Season the skin side with salt and leave covered on a plate at room temperature for 30 minutes.

Put the membrillo, sherry vinegar and garlic into a small food processor, add a quarter of the walnuts, ¼ teaspoon of salt and a few grinds of coarse black pepper. Blitz to a fairly smooth purée, wiping down the bowl several times as you do so. Transfer into a jar or bowl.

Heat a large frying pan (skillet) over a medium heat. Brush the skin side of the duck breasts (fillets) with the oil, then place them into the heated pan, skin side down, and cook until they have become quite golden and the fat has rendered out. Move them around from time to time, but don't turn them over. This will take about 10–12 minutes. If they're burning, reduce the heat. Carefully drain all but 1 tablespoon of the rendered fat from the pan into a heatproof bowl — this can be used later for roasting potatoes or the like. Turn them over carefully and cook for an additional 2–5 minutes, depending on how thick the breasts (fillets) are (they are best eaten a little pink). Remove the duck from the pan to a warm plate and put in a warm place.

Cook the figs in the cooking fat in the pan, cut side facing down, until caramelized. Turn over and cook for an additional 20 seconds.

To serve, lay the salad leaves onto warmed plates. Cut the duck breast (fillet) into slices 7mm (¼in.) thick and lay them on top. Dollop on the membrillo paste, then scatter on the figs, walnuts and grapes. Spoon a little of the pan juices on — they will be a bit fatty, but all the more delicious for it!

FOR 2 AS A MAIN COURSE

Confit duck leg, caramelized onions, almonds, porcini, cavolo nero and blue cheese

WARM

INGREDIENTS

2 confit duck legs

1 red onion, thinly sliced

1 garlic clove, sliced

2 tsp olive oil

2 tsp balsamic vinegar

150g (5½oz.) cavolo nero leaves (stalk removed), cut crossways into 2cm (¾in.) lengths

85g (3oz.) blue cheese (I used dolcelatte)

30g (1oz./2 tbsp) butter

150g (5½oz.) porcini mushrooms, cleaned and sliced

8 sage leaves, shredded

30g (1oz./3 tbsp) almonds, toasted and roughly chopped

Confit duck legs, a wonderful French invention, are completely delicious and you can find them at most delicatessens or French butchers. They are un-boned legs that have been salted for a day or two then cooked very slowly in duck fat. Once cooked by you at home they have lovely crispy skin and succulent firm flesh. You could serve roast chicken legs or breast (fillet) or duck breast (fillet) instead. The cavolo nero (which could be replaced with kale or spinach) and blue cheese purée is wonderfully good and a perfect match for lovely plump porcini mushrooms, or use another wild mushroom in season.

[METHOD]

Preheat the oven to 180°C (350°F/Gas mark 4). Line a roasting dish with baking parchment.

Put the duck legs in the oven for 6–8 minutes. By this point you should be able to cut and then gently remove the thigh and leg bones from the legs. Cut each leg into three or four pieces and return to the oven to crispen up for about 20 minutes.

Caramelize the onion and garlic in the olive oil over a medium heat with ¼ teaspoon of salt, stirring frequently. It will take about 8–10 minutes. Add the balsamic vinegar and cook until it has evaporated. Keep warm.

Boil or steam the cavolo nero in salted water for 3–4 minutes. Drain into a colander, then put into a small food processor or blender with half of the blue cheese. Pulse-blitz, adding hot water if needed, to give a purée – I prefer mine to have a little texture. Season with salt and pepper and keep warm.

Melt the butter in a frying pan (skillet) and sauté the porcini mushrooms with the sage until nicely coloured on both sides. Add the almonds and warm through. Season to taste.

Break the remainder of the blue cheese into pieces. To serve, spoon the cavolo nero purée onto warmed plates and spread it out. Lay the duck pieces and caramelized onion on top, then spoon on the porcini and scatter over the cheese.

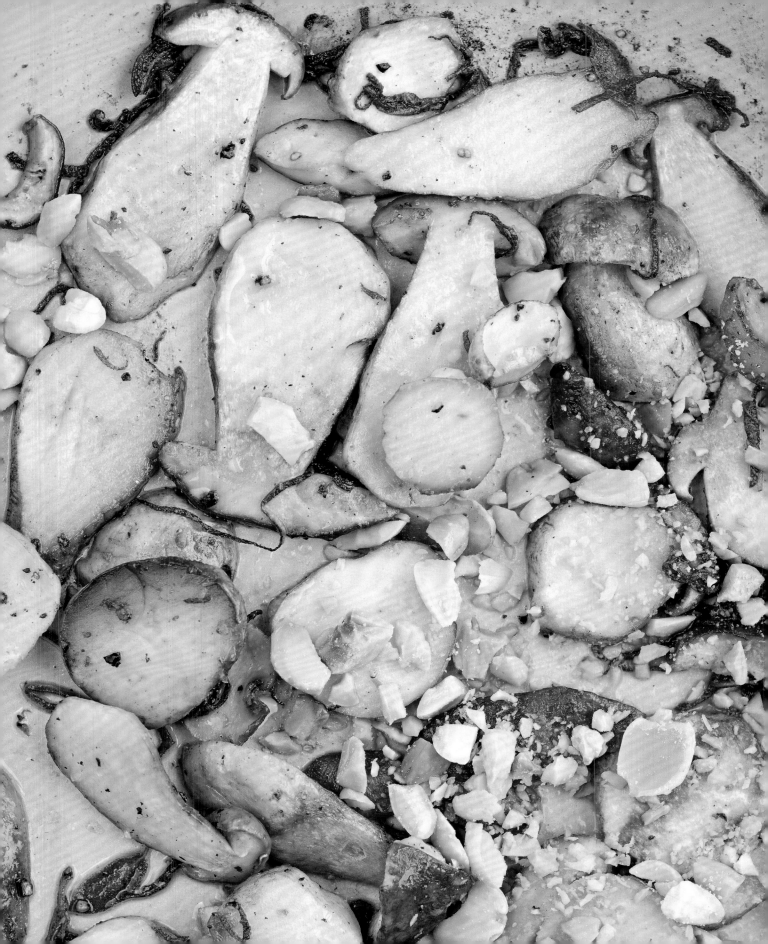

Steamed guinea fowl, spiced roast pumpkin and honeyed pecans

WARM OR AT ROOM TEMPERATURE

INGREDIENTS

4 guinea fowl (game hen) breasts (fillets), skin on or off

1 tbsp chopped mixed herbs (thyme, rosemary, sage, oregano)

2 tbsp olive oil

100g (3½oz./⅔ cup) pecans

2 tbsp honey

600g (1lb. 5oz.) pumpkin flesh, thickly sliced

1 tsp fennel seeds

1 tsp nigella seeds

½ tsp chilli flakes

½ tsp five-spice powder

1 large handful watercress, picked

100g (3½oz./scant ½ cup) egg-free milk aioli (see page 266)

This is a really good dish in autumn (the fall), when pumpkin is at its best. The slightly sweet flavour of pecans is even better when candied with honey, or even with maple or agave syrup. The egg-free milk aioli on page 266, which is made with black garlic, is terrific with this, but you could also serve it with plain aioli or even the honey mustard dressing on page 256.

[METHOD]

Preheat the oven to 160°C (325°F/Gas mark 3). Line a small baking sheet with baking parchment.

Sprinkle the guinea fowl (game hen) all over with the herbs and season lightly with salt and pepper. Leave covered in a cool place for 30 minutes. Just before steaming them, brush all over with 1 teaspoon of the oil.

Put the pecans and honey in a small saucepan and bring to the boil. Cook until the honey begins to caramelize, then tip onto the prepared baking sheet. Bake until golden – about 15–18 minutes, but keep an eye on it. Remove from the oven and increase the oven temperature to 180°C (350°F/Gas mark 4).

In a roasting dish, toss the pumpkin with the fennel and nigella seeds, chilli flakes, five-spice powder, a pinch of salt and the remaining oil. Roast until cooked through and golden, about 20 minutes, turning them once as they cook.

Put a steamer on and place the guinea fowl (game hen) breasts (fillets) in, making sure they don't overlap. Cook until done, about 7 minutes. (To test, cut a small slice from the thickest part – the meat should be almost fully cooked.) Turn off the heat and leave to rest in the steamer for 1 minute before removing.

To serve, lay the roast pumpkin and watercress on warmed plates. Slice each guinea fowl (game hen) breast (fillet) into four and lay on top. Scatter with the pecans. Serve with aioli.

Meat

CHAPTER 7

Seared beef rump, buttered scorzonera, girolles and edamame

WARM

INGREDIENTS

600g (1lb. 5oz.) beef rump (round)

2 tbsp olive oil

3 tbsp white vinegar

400g (14oz.) scorzonera or salsify root

30g (1oz./2 tbsp) butter

2 garlic cloves, thinly sliced

1 tbsp finely chopped or grated ginger

1 tsp fresh thyme leaves

1 tbsp lemon juice

1 large shallot, diced

200g (7oz.) girolle mushrooms, cleaned

150g (5½oz./1⅔ cups) podded edamame beans (or broad/fava beans or peas)

150g (5½oz.) baby spinach (or large leaf spinach)

Scorzonera, also known as black salsify, can be used interchangeably with 'normal' salsify. Both are quirky root vegetables that are grown in free-draining soil or sand so that the roots grow straight and long. Once washed, scorzonera has very dark, almost black skin (see page 1); once peeled, the flesh discolours quickly, so you'll need to either rub it with lemon juice, put it in acidulated water or wash the grit off, boil and then peel once cooked. Beef rump (round) has a lovely texture and flavour, but you could use any beef, lamb or pork steak here. Use whatever mushrooms are in season, or even a mixture of cultivated ones.

[METHOD]

Season the beef lightly on both sides with salt and pepper and brush with 1 tablespoon of the oil. Cover and leave at room temperature.

Bring a medium pan of salted water to the boil. Add the vinegar and turn off the heat. Wash the scorzonera of any grit, top and tail, then peel off the skin using a potato peeler and cut into lengths of about 10cm (4in.). As soon as each root is prepared, drop it into the water. Once all have been prepped, bring the water back to a gentle boil and cook until you can just insert a sharp knife through the centre of them, about 8–10 minutes. Drain.

Place a medium pan on a medium heat. Add the butter, garlic and ginger and cook, stirring, until it begins to caramelize. Add the scorzonera and thyme, salt and pepper and cook with the lid on until golden all over, stirring frequently to stop them catching. Add the lemon juice and keep warm.

Meanwhile, heat a wide frying pan (skillet) and sauté the shallot in the remaining 1 tablespoon of olive oil until soft and just beginning to colour. Add the girolle mushrooms, season with salt and pepper and cook over a medium heat until the mushrooms collapse a little and any liquid in the pan has boiled away. Stir in the edamame and keep warm.

Heat a frying pan (skillet) or griddle over a high heat. Cook the beef for 3 minutes, then turn it over and cook to your preferred doneness. (If, like me, you prefer it rare, it will need just another 90 seconds on the other side.) Rest it in a warm place for 8 minutes before slicing 1cm (½in.) thick.

If you cooked the beef in a frying pan (skillet), then add the spinach to it and cook to wilt it down briefly in the pan juices. If you cooked the beef on a griddle or barbecue, sauté the spinach briefly in a little oil or butter and season it.

To serve, divide the spinach among heated plates. Lay the scorzonera on top, then the beef. Scatter on the mushrooms and edamame and finish with flaky salt.

Miso and cacao marinated beef onglet with beans, soba noodles and avocado

WARM OR AT ROOM TEMPERATURE

Onglet is one of those delicious cuts of beef that for years few had even heard of in English-speaking countries, yet it now appears on menus from Britain to New Zealand. The term is French, but in the USA it's known as hanger steak so you may have eaten it before. I've happily tasted it numerous times in New York, Chicago and around California – always cooked rare, with fries and mustard mayonnaise, or a tomato-based salsa. It's a delicious cut, but is tender only if cooked rare. If you prefer your meat well done, then use either rump (round) or fillet. Ideally, marinate the beef for between 24 and 48 hours. This miso marinade is a Japanese creation called den miso, which traditionally doesn't include cacao. This version is based on a menu I co-created with Paul A. Young, British chocolate maestro, at The Providores in 2015. Cacao nibs are the seeds or beans from cacao (or cocoa) pods that have been fermented and dried, and usually, but not always, roasted. They are crunchy, slightly bitter and delicious – rather like dark chocolate. You can source them from a good food store or online. If they've not already been toasted, bake them on a tray in an oven preheated to 160°C (325°F/Gas mark 3) for 15 minutes, then cool. You can get 100% buckwheat soba noodles but I prefer ones made with a mixture of buckwheat and wheat flour as they're more supple. Replace them with vermicelli noodles or another pasta shape if you prefer.

INGREDIENTS

800g (1lb. 12oz.) beef onglet (hanger steak), about 650–700g (1lb. 7oz.–1lb. 9oz.) trimmed weight

100g (3½oz.) dried soba noodles

2 tsp sesame oil (or use sunflower or other plain oil)

1 large avocado

1 tbsp creamed horseradish or mustard

1 tbsp lime juice

150g (5½oz.) beans, trimmed, blanched and refreshed (I used a mixture of green and yellow beans)

2 tsp sesame seeds, toasted

2 tsp thinly sliced chives

FOR THE MISO MARINADE

100g (3½oz./generous ⅓ cup) pale miso paste (I used shiromiso – white miso – which is slightly sweet and savoury)

3½ tbsp sake (or use dry sherry, pale lager or apple juice)

85ml (⅓ cup) mirin

3½ tbsp caster (superfine) sugar

2 tbsp toasted cacao nibs, coarsely crushed

2 tsp finely chopped or grated ginger

[METHOD]

First make the miso marinade. In a heavy-based small pan, stir or whisk the miso paste with the sake, mirin and sugar until you have a sloppy paste. Place on a low heat and slowly bring to a gentle simmer, stirring the whole time. Increase the heat to medium and cook for 4 minutes until it thickens like tomato sauce. Stir in 1 tablespoon of the cacao nibs and the ginger, and cook for an additional 20 seconds, then remove from the heat, tip into a bowl and leave to cool.

Once the marinade has cooled completely, add the beef. Rub the marinade evenly over it, then cover tightly and store in the fridge. Turn the beef every

[RECIPE CONTINUES]

[RECIPE CONTINUED]

12 hours or so. Remove it from the fridge 90 minutes before you're going to cook it so it isn't cold in the centre.

Drop the soba noodles into a large pan half-filled with lightly salted boiling water. Bring back to the boil, then stir in 200ml (¾ cup) of cold water. Do this once more as soon as the water comes back to the boil, then lower the heat to medium and cook until the noodles are al dente. Drain into a colander and rinse until cool under running water. Tip into a large bowl and toss with ½ teaspoon of the sesame oil and leave at room temperature.

Remove the flesh from the avocado and mash it with the creamed horseradish and lime juice. Add salt and pepper to taste, cover with cling film (plastic wrap) and leave at room temperature.

Place a frying pan (skillet) or heavy-based pan over a medium–high heat. Wipe excess marinade from the beef, but leave about 10 per cent of it clinging to the meat. Brush with the remaining sesame oil. Place in the pan and cook for 3 minutes. It will begin to blacken in places because the sugar in the marinade will caramelize and blacken, but don't let the meat burn (turn it over sooner if necessary). Cook on the other side for 2 minutes. Remove the beef from the pan to a plate and leave to rest in a warm place for 5 minutes or so. (If your onglet has been butterflied it will take much less time to cook so do keep an eye on it.)

To serve, toss the soba noodles with the beans and divide among four plates. Dollop on the avocado mixture. Slice the beef against the grain, then lay this on top. Scatter on the sesame seeds, chives and the remaining cacao nibs.

FOR 4 AS A STARTER

Beef carpaccio, blackened green tomatoes, peppers, crispy ginger, Sichuan chilli oil and crispy garlic

ROOM TEMPERATURE

INGREDIENTS

300g (10½oz.) fillet steak, trimmed of all fat and sinew

1 red (bell) pepper

1 yellow (bell) pepper

2 tbsp olive oil

vegetable oil for deep-frying

5cm (2in.) piece ginger, peeled then cut into fine matchsticks

6 garlic cloves, thinly sliced

1 medium–hot red chilli

4 Sichuan peppercorns, crushed

2 green tomatoes, thinly sliced

1 tbsp thinly sliced chives

Beef carpaccio is a dish from Venice, named in honour of the Venetian painter Vittore Carpaccio, whose paintings have a lovely way with the colour red – especially deep blood-reds – which is perhaps why this raw beef dish was named after him. Here, I serve this dish in an altogether non-Venetian way – with tongue-numbing Sichuan peppercorns from China and crispy ginger. This is quite a rich dish so I'd suggest it makes a better starter than a main course. Green (i.e. unripe) tomatoes have a lovely acidity to them, and when blackened they take on some smoky notes, which works really well with the rest of the ingredients. You can barbecue the peppers to remove their skin, or cook them as described here, under a grill (broiler).

[METHOD]

The beef will be easiest to slice if slightly frozen, so wrap it up tightly in cling film (plastic wrap) and place it in the freezer for 40 minutes to help it keep its shape.

Prepare the peppers. Heat the grill (broiler) to full and sit an oven rack 8–10cm (3–4in.) under the heat. Cut the peppers lengthways into halves or quarters, depending on their size and shape. Remove the seeds and stems, then, skin facing up, press them flat using the palm of your hand. Lay them in a shallow roasting dish and brush the skins with 1 teaspoon of the olive oil. Grill (broil) until the skins blister and blacken, about 3–6 minutes. Place the peppers in a bowl, cover with cling film (plastic wrap) and leave to cool (or place in an oven bag and fold in on itself). Once they've cooled, peel off the skins and slice into strips.

In a small pan, heat 3cm (1¼in.) of the vegetable oil to 160°C (325°F) and deep-fry the ginger until it curls, darkens and crisps up. Remove with a slotted spoon and drain on absorbent kitchen paper.

Cook the garlic in the same way, being careful not to burn it or it will become bitter.

Slice half the chilli into rings and deep-fry these in the same way.

Discard the stem from the rest of the chilli and finely chop it, along with its seeds. Place in a small pan with the Sichuan peppercorns. Add the remaining olive oil

[RECIPE CONTINUES]

[RECIPE CONTINUED]

and place over a medium heat, then cook until the chilli sizzles. Cook for 1 minute, then remove from the heat and tip into a heatproof bowl to cool.

Heat a frying pan (skillet) and cook the tomato slices, without any oil, until blackened on both sides. Remove from the pan and lay on a plate.

Slice the beef. You'll find it easier to slice still wrapped up in the cling film (plastic wrap), which you can then peel off after slicing it. Cut it as thin as you can using a very sharp knife and lay the slices on a tray. If the slices are too thick, you can gently bash them between a double layer of cling film (plastic wrap) or baking parchment.

To serve, alternate slices of beef and green tomatoes on the plates. Sprinkle with a little flaky salt. Criss-cross the pepper strips on top and drizzle with the chilli oil. Scatter on the crispy ginger, chilli slices, garlic and chives.

Poached veal, anchovy aioli and potatoes

SLIGHTLY CHILLED OR AT ROOM TEMPERATURE

INGREDIENTS

800g (1lb. 12oz.) veal silverside (round), trimmed of any sinew

2 litres (8½ cups) veal stock (or chicken or light beef stock)

1 tbsp fish sauce

2 bay leaves

10cm (4in.) rosemary sprig

5 thyme sprigs

1 tbsp oregano leaves

800g (1lb. 12oz.) small waxy potatoes

1 small handful flat-leaf (Italian) parsley leaves, coarsely shredded

2 spring onions (scallions), thinly sliced

2 handfuls rocket (arugula)

1 large juicy lemon, cut into wedges

FOR THE ANCHOVY AIOLI

4 salted anchovy fillets, gently rinsed under cold water to remove salt crystals and bones (or 6 anchovy fillets in oil)

1 egg

1 garlic clove (I used smoked)

1 tbsp English mustard

1 tbsp white vinegar (cider, white wine or rice vinegar)

250ml (1 cup) olive oil

This is based on the classic Piedmontese dish Vitello tonnato, *cold braised veal topped with a tuna-based mayonnaise. I've tweaked the original dish and served the veal with an anchovy aioli and potato salad instead. Veal need no longer be something to frown at, so long as you use rose veal or equivalent, which means the young male calves have had a decent, albeit short, life. I used silverside (round), but you could also use loin or fillet. I made the aioli with smoked garlic but you could use plain garlic and season it with smoked salt, if you wish. Using a whole egg in the aioli will guarantee it won't split.*

[METHOD]

Tie the veal fairly tightly with string, or ask your butcher to do so. (This helps keep it close-knit when poaching and allows it to cook evenly.) Lightly season all over with salt. Choose a saucepan that will comfortably hold the veal.

Bring the stock to the boil with the fish sauce, bay leaves, rosemary, thyme and oregano. Carefully lower the veal into the simmering stock. It needs to be submerged, so top up with boiling water if necessary. Bring the stock back to the boil, then reduce to a simmer for 5 minutes. Turn the veal over, turn off the heat and put a lid on the pan. For medium–rare veal, leave in the liquid for 10–15 minutes, depending on the circumference of the veal. Remove from the stock, reserving the stock, and leave to cool on a plate, then cover and refrigerate for up to 48 hours. Just before serving it, take it out of the fridge and remove the string.

Add the potatoes to the stock, bring back to the boil, then cook until done. Leave to cool for 10 minutes, then drain in a colander.

Meanwhile, make the anchovy aioli. In a small food processor, pulse-blitz the anchovies, egg, garlic, mustard, vinegar and ¼ teaspoon of salt to a paste. Keeping the motor running, slowly pour in the oil until all has been absorbed. Taste for seasoning, adding extra vinegar if needed. Slice the potatoes 1cm (½in.) thick and toss with the parsley, spring onions (scallions) and a third of the aioli.

To serve, thinly slice the veal and divide among chilled plates. Scatter on the rocket (arugula) and spoon on the potato salad. Drizzle with more aioli and coarsely grind lots of black pepper over it. Serve with lemon wedges.

Lamb loin, crispy kale, aubergine, shiitake, mint, yogurt and sumac

WARM

INGREDIENTS

700g (1lb. 9oz.) lamb loin, excess fat and sinew removed (but leave a little fat), at room temperature

vegetable oil for deep-frying the kale

150g (5½oz.) kale, stem removed, washed and patted dry

3 tbsp olive oil

1 large aubergine (eggplant), stem removed, sliced lengthways 5mm (¼in.) thick

1 tsp fennel seeds

1 tsp roughly chopped rosemary leaves

150g (5½oz.) shiitake mushrooms, stalks removed

1 tsp soy sauce

1 tbsp extra virgin olive oil

20 mint leaves, large ones shredded, smaller ones left whole

1 tsp sumac

150ml (⅔ cup) Greek-style plain yogurt

This combination is a bit of a mash-up of the Middle East and Japan. I've used loin here, but neck fillet, a leg chop or even some pulled slow-braised shoulder would work well. You could steam the kale for this dish but it really is worth the effort of deep-frying it.

[METHOD]

Preheat the oven to 160°C (325°F/Gas mark 3). Line one or two baking sheets with absorbent kitchen paper. Season the lamb with salt and pepper.

In a deep pan, heat 4cm (1½in.) of vegetable oil to 170°C (340°F). Add a few kale leaves at a time and deep-fry until crisp but before they turn brown, removing them from the oil with tongs or a slotted spoon to drain on absorbent kitchen paper. Lay the kale in a single layer on the prepared baking sheet(s) and dry off in the oven for about 10 minutes. As soon as it's fully crisp, remove from the oven and leave to cool. Increase the oven temperature to 180°C (350°F/Gas mark 4).

Heat up a heavy-based pan. Brush the lamb with 2 teaspoons of the olive oil, then sear the meat until brown on all sides. Remove to a roasting dish and cook in the oven for about 5–6 minutes for rare lamb, 7–9 for medium rare or 12 minutes for medium, depending on the thickness of the loin. Remove from the oven and leave to rest for at least 10 minutes in a warm place.

Meanwhile, cook the aubergine (eggplant). Brush on both sides with 2 tablespoons of the oil. Heat up a griddle or heavy-based frying pan (skillet) over a medium–high heat and cook the aubergine (eggplant), a few slices at a time, until cooked through, about 2 minutes on each side. Stack on a plate and keep warm.

Heat the remaining 1 teaspoon of oil over a medium heat in a medium pan with the fennel seeds and rosemary until the seeds begin to turn golden. Stir in the shiitake mushrooms, add the soy sauce and 1 tablespoon of water and cover the pan. Cook over a low heat until the mushrooms have collapsed a little and are cooked through, stirring twice. Turn off the heat and keep warm.

In a small bowl, stir the extra virgin olive oil, shredded mint and half the sumac into the yogurt. To serve, lay the aubergine (eggplant) slices on warmed plates. Slice the lamb, against the grain, and lay this on top. Sit the shiitake and crispy kale on top, then dollop on the yogurt. Scatter with the mint leaves and remaining sumac.

233

Lamb neck, baked pita, figs, feta, tomato, cucumber, mint and Kalamata olives

WARM

This salad was one of the most popular of the photo shoot; in fact, it smelled so good that we ate it as a mid-morning snack! I used lamb neck fillet – a personal favourite cut – but you could also use lamb loin, leg steaks or even leftover slices of roast leg of lamb. Black olives work better than green ones in this dish.

INGREDIENTS

900g (2lb.) lamb neck fillet, trimmed of excess fat and sinew

4 tbsp extra virgin olive oil

3 or 4 pita breads, depending on size, torn into pieces

2 tbsp red wine vinegar

150g (5½oz./about ¾ cup) Kalamata olives

4 tomatoes

2 small cucumbers, peeled and sliced

30 mint leaves, torn

200g (7oz.) feta cheese (ideally 100% ewes' milk), roughly crumbled

½ tsp dried oregano

6 figs

1 juicy lemon, cut into six wedges

[METHOD]

Preheat the oven to 170°C (350°F/Gas mark 4). Place a roasting dish on your hob (stove) on a medium heat or, if you're roasting in a ceramic or Pyrex dish, place a frying pan (skillet) on the heat.

Season the lamb with salt and pepper and brush with 1 teaspoon of the oil. Put it in the heated roasting dish or frying pan (skillet) and cook until well browned on all sides. Remove the lamb and add the pita bread, tossing it around to coat in the fats. Sit the lamb on the bread in the roasting dish and roast in the oven until the lamb is cooked. Because lamb neck can be a little fatty, cooking it medium works best here. Neck fillets will take about 10 minutes. Remove the lamb to another dish and leave to rest in a warm place for 10 minutes, then slice it and put it on a plate, reserving the cooking juices.

Drizzle the vinegar over the pita, add the olives and half the remaining olive oil and toss together. Bake until the bread is crisp, about 8–10 minutes, then remove from the oven.

While the bread is baking, cut the tomatoes in half crossways, then gently squeeze out and discard the seeds. Cut the flesh into chunks and mix with the cucumber, mint, feta, oregano and remaining olive oil.

Remove the stems from the figs, and peel if you like, then thickly slice and add to the tomato salad. Toss everything together and season lightly with salt (the feta will be salty) and coarsely grind on ¼ teaspoon of black pepper.

To serve, pile the tomato salad on top of the crisp pita. Lay the lamb on top and drizzle over the cooking juices. Serve with the lemon wedges.

Cardamom lamb ribs, mango-cashew rice and red onions

WARM

INGREDIENTS

2kg (4½lb.) lamb ribs

2 red onions, halved

1 carrot, thickly sliced

12 green cardamom pods, smashed in mortar and pestle

1 cinnamon stick

¼ tsp coarsely ground black pepper

½ vanilla pod (bean), slit lengthways

85ml (⅓ cup) vinegar (any type will work)

4 tbsp agave syrup (or use honey or maple syrup)

400g (14oz./2¾ cups) red Camargue rice

1 tsp cumin seeds, toasted

1 mango, peeled, flesh removed and diced

2 spring onions (scallions), thinly sliced

100g (3½oz./⅔ cup) cashews, toasted and roughly chopped

½ green chilli, chopped

4 tbsp lemon juice

½ tsp finely grated lemon zest

Lamb ribs may not be as well known as pork or beef ribs, but they are absolutely delicious. They're a little fatty, but pre-cooking, by simmering, helps to remove some of this fat. This is definitely a family or friends meal – there's nothing at all fancy here.

[METHOD]

Place the ribs in your largest pan, cut to fit. Thickly slice one of the onions and put it in the pan with the carrot, 10 cardamom pods, the cinnamon stick, black pepper, vanilla pod (bean), vinegar and 2 teaspoons of salt. Cover with cold water and slowly bring to the boil. Place a cartouche on top, cover with a tight-fitting lid and simmer for 2 hours.

Leave the ribs to cool in the stock, then cut into portions of two or three ribs. Put 200ml (¾ cup) of the cooking liquor and all the solids from the stock into a saucepan with the remaining two cardamom pods and the agave syrup. Bring to the boil and reduce by half.

Preheat the oven to 180°C (350°F/Gas mark 4). Line a shallow roasting dish with baking parchment.

Cook the rice. Rinse it in a sieve and put it in a medium saucepan with the cumin, ½ teaspoon of salt and 800ml (3⅓ cups) of water. Bring to the boil, then put a lid on and simmer for 18 minutes. Turn off the heat and leave to cool in the saucepan. Once cooled, tip into a large bowl and mix with the mango, spring onions (scallions) and half the cashews.

Thinly slice the remaining onion and mix with the chilli, lemon juice and zest and ¼ teaspoon of salt.

Place the ribs in the roasting dish and pour on the reduced cooking stock. Roast the ribs until bubbling and golden. The longer you cook them the stickier they'll be.

To serve, pile the rice salad on a platter. Sit the lamb ribs on top, then scatter on the onion and remaining cashews.

Lambs' kidneys, roast sweet potato, orange and prunes with smoked paprika mayonnaise

WARM

INGREDIENTS

2 orange-fleshed sweet potatoes (800–900g/ 1¾–2lb.) – don't peel them

1 tbsp olive oil

6 prunes (about 125g/4½oz.), pitted and quartered

1 orange, segmented and each segment cut into thirds

1½ tsp smoked paprika – dulce (sweet) rather than piquante (hot), if you have it

140g (5oz./⅔ cup) mayonnaise or egg-free milk aioli (see pages 264 and 266 respectively)

3 tbsp flour

1 tsp chopped rosemary

12 lambs' kidneys (about 900g/2lb.), cleaned and halved

50g (1¾oz./⅓ cup) butter

6 spring onions (scallions), cut into 5cm (2in.) lengths

3½ tbsp crème fraîche (thick sour cream)

1 handful salad leaves (I used baby kale, but watercress or baby spinach would work well)

OK, not everyone will enjoy the taste of a kidney. If you prefer, you can replace them with livers (chicken, veal, pork or lamb), brains (oh, yes please!) or, if you're not a fan of offal in any form, lamb neck fillet cut into slices 2cm (¾in.) thick.

[METHOD]

Preheat the oven to 180°C (350°F/Gas mark 4). Line a baking sheet with baking parchment.

Boil the unpeeled sweet potatoes in salted water until you can almost insert a knife the whole way through, about 15 minutes. Carefully remove them from the pan with tongs to a colander and leave to cool for 10 minutes. Cut off the pointed ends, then slice 1cm (½in.) thick and lay them on the prepared baking sheet. Drizzle with the oil, sprinkle with salt and pepper and roast until golden, about 25 minutes.

Mix the prunes and orange together along with any juice you can squeeze from the orange core.

In a small bowl, stir half the smoked paprika into the mayonnaise, adding some salt if needed.

In a large bowl, mix the flour and rosemary with the remaining smoked paprika and 1 teaspoon of salt. Add the kidneys and toss in the flour. Leave for 5 minutes.

Heat a pan with half the butter. Add the spring onions (scallions) and cook for 1 minute, tossing until they colour a little. Remove from the pan and keep warm. Add the remaining butter to the pan and add the kidneys, cut side down. You may need to do this in two batches. Cook over a medium heat for 2 minutes, then turn and cook for an additional minute, or a bit longer if you don't want them pink. Add the crème fraîche (thick sour cream) along with the spring onions (scallions). Bring to the boil, taste for seasoning, then reduce the heat and simmer for 1 minute.

To serve, place the sweet potatoes on a warm platter or plates and scatter with the salad leaves. Spoon on the kidneys, spring onions (scallions) and sauce, then the prunes and orange. Serve with the smoked paprika mayonnaise.

Jamón ibérico, peaches, mozzarella and purple pesto

AT ROOM TEMPERATURE

INGREDIENTS

1 handful wild rocket (arugula)

3 or 4 peaches (I used doughnut peaches as they were the best on the day)

250g (9oz.) bocconcini mozzarella

100g (3½oz.) jamón ibérico, thinly sliced

6 edible flowers for garnish (optional)

FOR THE PURPLE PESTO

1 small garlic clove, crushed

¼ tsp finely grated lemon zest

20 purple basil leaves

3 tbsp pine nuts, lightly toasted

20g (¾oz./¾ tbsp) finely grated Parmesan cheese

3 tbsp extra virgin olive oil

2 tsp lemon juice

The key here is to make sure every ingredient is perfect: the peaches need to be ripe and sweet and the mozzarella should be the best you can get – ideally, mozzarella di buffala. I used the small mozzarella balls called bocconcini, which look great, but you could simply tear larger ones into smaller pieces. I also used one of the world's great ingredients in this: jamón ibérico de bellota. It's a fabulous rich cured pork leg from Spain, where you'll also source jamón Serrano. I like the former so much that I set up a restaurant in Auckland in 2006 called Bellota in honour of the acorns (bellota) that these fabulous pigs feast on. Italian prosciutto can also be used successfully with this combination. To bring it all together, make this purple pesto – but if green basil is all you have, then use that, of course. Make the pesto with a mortar and pestle, or use a small food processor. The volume isn't large, so if you make it in anything bigger, it'll likely not form the consistency you want. I had some violas growing in the garden so threw those on as well.

[METHOD]

Make the purple pesto. Pound the garlic and lemon zest with ¼ teaspoon of salt using a mortar and pestle. Pound in the basil four leaves at a time (any more and they will fly out of the mortar). Add the pine nuts and pound to a chunky consistency, then mix in the Parmesan, olive oil and lemon juice. Taste for seasoning.

To serve, scatter the rocket (arugula) on your platter. Cut the peaches in half, remove the stone (pit), cut into wedges and place on top of the rocket (arugula). Gently pull each bocconcini almost in half to expose their centres and sit them among the peaches. Lay the jamón on, tucking it in loosely, then dollop on the pesto. Finally, scatter with the edible flowers, if using.

Roast lardons, sweet potato, chickpeas and runner beans

WARM

INGREDIENTS

200g (7oz.) lardons

1 tbsp olive oil

1 small red onion, halved and thinly sliced

3 garlic cloves, thinly sliced

1 tbsp freshly chopped thyme, rosemary or sage, or a mixture

1kg (2lb. 4oz.) sweet potatoes, peeled and cut into chunks

250g (9oz./1½ cups) cooked chickpeas (a 400g/14oz. can chickpeas gives you roughly this amount)

300g (10½oz.) runner (pole) beans, strings removed, topped and tailed then cut on an angle

For those unfamiliar with them, lardons are smallish diced or baton-shaped pieces of smoked or unsmoked bacon. In France they go in everything from frisée (curly endive) salads with goats' cheese to Coq au Vin or Quiche Lorraine. If you can't buy them, simply cut thickly sliced streaky (belly) bacon into pieces. This is good served as a hearty starter in cooler months and it can also be served as the carbohydrate component in a main meal with roast fish or poultry on top. For brunch, serve it with a poached egg. To cook dried chickpeas see page 79, or use canned ones, drained and rinsed.

[METHOD]

Preheat the oven to 175°C (350°F/Gas mark 4).

Place a saucepan over a medium heat and after a minute add the lardons and the oil. Sauté until they begin to colour, stirring to prevent them sticking. Add the onion, garlic and herbs and continue to cook until the onion has collapsed and is beginning to caramelize.

Put the sweet potato and chickpeas into a roasting dish and add the lardon mixture. Add 1 teaspoon of salt and ¼ teaspoon of coarsely ground black pepper and toss everything together. Roast, stirring from time to time, until the sweet potatoes are cooked and slightly coloured, about 25 minutes.

Just before the end of this time, blanch the beans in salted water and drain.

To serve, toss the beans with the sweet potato and lardons and taste for seasoning.

FOR 4 AS A BRUNCH DISH

Sausage, potato, fennel and watercress with a fried egg

WARM

INGREDIENTS

750g (1lb. 10oz.) sausages (8–10 depending on their size)

2 heads fennel (500g/ 1lb. 2oz.), trimmed and thinly sliced lengthways

1 tsp fennel seeds

12 sage leaves, coarsely shredded

1 tbsp extra virgin olive oil

600g (1lb. 5oz.) small potatoes

4 eggs

2 tbsp butter (or use olive oil)

1 large handful watercress, any thick or woody stalks discarded

You can use any flavour sausage for this very simple weekend brunch dish, but one of my favourites is pork and fennel. The North African non-pork, lamb-based merguez are delicious but will need no boiling and only half the roasting time as they are much thinner. I boil my sausages before baking them as I like what it does to their texture, and it removes a little of their fat, but you can skip this step if you find it a bit of a faff. You can use any small potatoes, waxy or floury, or large ones cut into chunks.

[METHOD]

Preheat the oven to 170°C (350°F/Gas mark 4).

Separate the sausages from each other and place in a saucepan large enough to hold them all comfortably and cover with cold water. Bring to the boil then reduce the heat to a simmer and cook for 1 minute. Drain in a colander. While still hot, cut into slices 2cm (¾in.) thick.

Place the sausage pieces in a roasting dish with the fennel, fennel seeds, sage and olive oil. Toss everything together and roast, stirring occasionally, until the fennel colours, about 20 minutes.

Meanwhile, boil the potatoes in salted water until cooked. Drain into a colander and mix into the sausage mixture.

Fry the eggs in the butter to your liking — I always prefer a runny yolk.

To serve, lay the watercress on four warmed plates and scatter over the sausage and potato mixture. Sit a fried egg on top.

FOR 2 AS A MAIN COURSE

Pork chop, watermelon and pomelo with coconut sauce

MEAT WARM, SALAD AT ROOM TEMPERATURE

INGREDIENTS

400–500g (14oz.–1lb. 2oz.) pork chop on the bone

200ml (¾ cup + 2 tsp) coconut milk

½ red chilli, chopped

1 garlic clove, finely chopped

7.5cm (3in.) lemongrass stem from the lower end, two outer layers discarded, insides thinly sliced

1 tsp fish sauce (or use soy sauce or salt)

1 shallot, chopped

85g (3oz.) pomelo flesh

1 tbsp goji berries

¼ tsp finely grated lime zest

4 tbsp lime juice

300g (10½oz.) watermelon flesh, cut into wedges

1 small inner celery stalk, thinly sliced, including the leaves

olive oil, for brushing

30g (1oz./½ cup) coconut chips or long threads, toasted

1 spring onion (scallion), thinly sliced

The great thing about this salad, apart from the popping flavours, is that the watermelon and pomelo combo is a fantastic vegetarian salad in its own right. Pomelo are very large citrus fruit. Although it can be quite hard to peel and separate the flesh unless you use a knife, they're crunchy and not as sour as grapefruit. If you can't find them, then use pink grapefruit.

[METHOD]

Preheat the oven to 180°C (350°F/Gas mark 4). Season the pork chop with salt and pepper and bring to room temperature on a plate.

Place the coconut milk, chilli, garlic, lemongrass and fish sauce in a small saucepan and heat until reduced by half. Keep warm.

Mix the shallot, pomelo and goji berries with the lime zest and juice and leave to macerate for 10 minutes. Mix in the watermelon and celery.

Brush the pork chop with oil and cook on a high heat in a heavy-based frying pan (skillet) until coloured and marked on both sides. Transfer to a roasting pan and roast in the oven until cooked — and this really will depend on the thickness of your chop or chops. To test if it's cooked, slice into the thickest part of the chop: if it's pink but not raw then it's ready. Remove from the oven and leave to rest in a warm place for 10 minutes.

To serve, divide the watermelon and pomelo salad among your plates. Cut the bone from the pork chop and slice the meat. Lay it over the top, then spoon on the warm coconut sauce. Sprinkle with the coconut chips and spring onion (scallion).

Previous pages: Cardamom lamb ribs
(left, see page 236) and pork chop (right).

Thai-style gammon hock, cucumber, papaya, toasted rice, macadamias and hot-and-sour tamarind caramel

MEAT WARM, SALAD AT ROOM TEMPERATURE

INGREDIENTS

2 gammon (ham) hocks (about 1.2kg/2lb. 10oz. each) or knuckle ends

3½ tbsp soy sauce

6 star anise

6 lime leaves

1 lemongrass stem, bashed and halved

2 red chillies, chopped (including seeds)

4 tbsp grated fresh ginger

6 garlic cloves, chopped

200g (7oz./1 cup) caster (superfine) sugar

3–4 tbsp tamarind paste (more or less to taste)

2 tsp fish sauce

2 tbsp white rice (any type)

2 carrots, peeled, then peeled into strips

1 cucumber, peeled, halved lengthways, deseeded and thinly sliced

1 x 400g (14oz.) papaya, peeled, seeds discarded, diced

1 shallot, thinly sliced into rings

1 medium bunch coriander (cilantro), picked

30 mint leaves, torn

100g (3½oz./¾ cup) macadamia nuts , toasted and chopped

This is a slightly time-consuming salad, but it's really worth the effort. The sticky twice-cooked gammon (ham) is really tasty, and your home will have delicious aromas of star anise! You can cook the gammon (ham) a few days beforehand so there's no need to feel rushed.

[METHOD]

Put the gammon (ham) hocks in a large saucepan and cover with cold water. Bring to the boil and cook for 2 minutes. Drain into a colander, then return to the saucepan and run cold water over them for 2 minutes. Drain again, then return to the saucepan and add the soy sauce, star anise, lime leaves, lemongrass, half the chopped chilli, half the ginger and half the garlic. Cover with water and bring to the boil. Cover with a cartouche, then simmer for 90 minutes. Tear a chunk of meat from the bone: if it comes away easily, then it's cooked; if not, cook a little longer. Leave to cool in the poaching liquor.

Remove the cool hocks from the stock and pull the fatty skin off and cut it into strips. Pull the flesh from the bones and break or cut into large pieces and place on a baking sheet lined with baking parchment. Strain 100ml (scant ½ cup) of the stock and reserve. (You can reduce the remainder by half and then freeze it for using in soups and stews.) Preheat the oven to 200°C (400°/Gas mark 6).

Cook the sugar in a medium saucepan over a medium–high heat until it caramelizes. (Stir briefly only if necessary to mix the melting sugar into the sugar granules.) Stir in the remaining chilli, ginger and garlic until incorporated. Add the tamarind paste, fish sauce and reserved stock and bring to the boil, then boil until syrupy. Pour one third of this syrup over the gammon (ham) and bake until golden and caramelized, about 20 minutes. Toss it several times as it cooks.

Meanwhile, dry-toast the rice in a pan over a medium heat until golden. Cool, then grind in a spice grinder or using a mortar and pestle. (Large pieces could break your tooth so make sure it's fairly fine.)

Mix the carrots, cucumber, papaya, shallot, coriander (cilantro) and mint together.

To serve, lay the papaya salad on your platter or plates. Place the gammon (ham) on, then spoon on the remaining dressing. Sprinkle with the toasted rice and nuts.

Venison, coconut-curried pumpkin and mustard cabbage

WARM

Venison is a fantastic meat both because of its flavour and because it is lean and healthy. Farmed venison is much less strong in flavour than wild venison – more like beef. The key when roasting any meat is to rest it once cooked for at least half the amount of time you cooked it. This ensures that the juices stay within the meat once sliced.

INGREDIENTS

4 x 150g (5½oz.) pieces of venison loin or leg steaks

¼ small Savoy cabbage (250g/9oz.), core removed and thinly shredded

1 tbsp English mustard

3 tbsp cider vinegar, or other white vinegar

1 tsp caster (superfine) sugar

500g (1lb. 2oz.) pumpkin flesh, cut into chunks

½ tsp cumin seeds

20 curry leaves

1 tbsp sesame oil

1 tbsp sunflower oil

1 red onion, halved and thinly sliced

2 star anise

2 garlic cloves, thinly sliced

5cm (2in.) piece ginger, peeled and cut into matchsticks or coarsely chopped or grated

1 red chilli, chopped

2 tsp fish sauce

5cm (2in.) lemongrass stem from the lower end, two outer layers discarded, insides thinly sliced

4 kaffir lime leaves

300ml (1¼ cups) coconut milk

[METHOD]

Preheat the oven to 170°C (350°F/Gas mark 4). Sit the venison on a plate, cover with cling film (plastic wrap) and leave to come to room temperature.

Put the shredded cabbage into a bowl. Mix the mustard, vinegar, sugar and ½ teaspoon of salt together, then pour over the cabbage and stir to coat. Cover the bowl and set aside.

Put the pumpkin in a roasting dish along with the cumin seeds and curry leaves. Drizzle on 1 teaspoon of the sesame oil and season with ½ teaspoon of salt. Toss together and bake for 10 minutes.

Meanwhile, place a medium pan over a medium heat. Add the sunflower oil, onion and star anise and cook until the onion begins to caramelize, stirring often. Add the garlic, ginger and chilli and cook for an additional 2 minutes, stirring. Add the fish sauce and cook for 30 seconds, then add the lemongrass, lime leaves and coconut milk and bring to the boil. Cook over a medium heat for 4 minutes.

Remove the roasting dish from the oven and pour the curry sauce over the pumpkin. Return to the oven and continue cooking until the pumpkin is cooked and coloured. Turn the oven off and keep the pumpkin warm in the oven.

Meanwhile, cook your venison. Place a heavy-based saucepan over a medium–high heat and wait until it gives off a blue haze. Brush the steaks with the remaining 2 teaspoons of sesame oil and lightly season with salt and pepper on both sides. Place the steaks in the pan and cook for 3 minutes. Turn over and cook to your preferred degree of doneness. (If you like it medium–rare, and the steaks are 3cm/1¼in. thick, they'll need just another 2 minutes.) Remove the steaks and rest them on a warm plate, covered with foil, for 5–8 minutes.

To serve, spoon the pumpkin onto four warmed plates and lay the cabbage across it. Slice the venison 1cm (½in.) thick and lay on top, then spoon over the sauce.

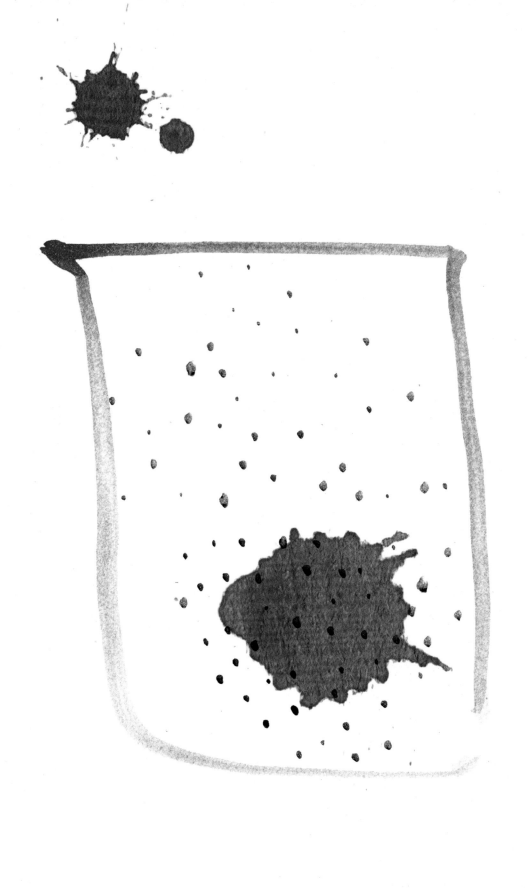

Dressings

CHAPTER 8

Honey mustard

INGREDIENTS

1½ tbsp runny honey

2 tbsp grain mustard

1 tbsp English mustard

2 tbsp lemon juice

100ml (scant ½ cup) extra virgin rapeseed oil (or sunflower or olive oil)

This can be used to dress a salad of thinly sliced ham, warm halved waxy potatoes, green beans and soft-boiled eggs, or a hot-smoked salmon and watercress salad scattered with toasted pumpkin seeds and cherry tomatoes. It will keep for 2 weeks if stored in the fridge.

[METHOD]

Whisk the honey and mustards together, then the lemon juice and finally the oil. You shouldn't need to add salt, but taste it to be sure.

Lemongrass, ginger and chilli

INGREDIENTS

5cm (2in.) lemongrass stem from the lower end, two outer layers discarded, insides thinly sliced

1 tbsp finely chopped or grated ginger

½ tsp lemon zest, finely grated

½ chilli, finely chopped (red or green)

1 tsp palm sugar (or unrefined caster/superfine sugar)

2 tsp fish sauce (or ¼ tsp salt)

120ml (½ cup) lemon juice

2 tbsp sunflower oil

This does not contain much oil compared with a more 'Western-style' dressing, and it goes really well on grilled (broiled) or steamed fish or chicken or tossed in with crisp raw vegetables. Use as much chilli as suits your taste. This dressing will keep in the fridge for 5 days, but it does lose its freshness.

[METHOD]

Put all the ingredients in a jar with a tight-fitting lid and shake well to combine. Leave for 30 minutes before tasting, adding a few tablespoons of cold water if it tastes too sharp.

Opposite, clockwise from top: Sesame, ginger and miso; Lemongrass, ginger and chilli; Sherry vinegar and pomegranate molasses; Honey mustard; Chia seeds, ginger, honey and lime.

Sherry vinegar and pomegranate molasses

INGREDIENTS

2 tbsp sherry vinegar

1½ tbsp pomegranate molasses

1 tsp soy sauce

½ garlic clove, finely chopped

100ml (scant ½ cup) extra virgin olive oil

This dressing really is a fusion of cultures, the Spanish sherry vinegar happily combining with Middle Eastern pomegranate molasses and Asian soy sauce. It goes really well drizzled over barbecued steaks or salmon, tossed with roast vegetables or used to dress grilled (broiled) mushrooms or asparagus. It will keep in the fridge for 2 weeks.

[METHOD]

Put the sherry vinegar, molasses, soy sauce and garlic in a jar with a tight-fitting lid and shake until the molasses has dissolved. Add the oil and shake again. Taste for seasoning, adding either more soy or some salt.

Chia seeds, ginger, honey and lime

INGREDIENTS

1 tbsp chia seeds

3 tbsp lime juice

1 tbsp finely chopped or grated ginger

1 tbsp agave syrup (or use runny honey or palm sugar)

150ml (⅔ cup) sunflower oil

Chia seeds are considered somewhat of a superfood and so here is a recipe that's easy to make and fairly versatile that you can use frequently. This is fabulous tossed with salad leaves, cucumber and tomatoes, or on a warm potato salad. Use it to dress chilled soba noodles, tofu and cold roast chicken. Blend it using either a stick blender or a small jug blender. It will keep in the fridge for 5 days.

[METHOD]

Mix the chia seeds with 4 tablespoons of water in a small bowl and leave to soak for 15 minutes. Mix with all the other ingredients and ¼ teaspoon of salt, then purée at high speed for 30 seconds. Taste for seasoning and add extra lime juice or salt as needed.

Sesame, ginger and miso

INGREDIENTS

90ml (6 tbsp) rice vinegar (or any other white vinegar)

2 tsp miso paste

1 tbsp finely chopped or grated ginger

1 tbsp tahini paste

1 tsp black sesame seeds (or use toasted white sesame)

4 tbsp toasted sesame oil

75ml (5 tbsp) sunflower oil

This thick but sharp dressing is lovely spooned over boiled rice and steamed greens, drizzled over grilled (broiled) asparagus or fish or tossed through a warm chicken salad. It also goes really well with chunks of warm roast pumpkin or beetroot (beet). It will keep in the fridge for 5 days.

[METHOD]

Whisk the vinegar, miso and ginger together to form a slurry. Mix in the tahini and sesame seeds. Whisk in the oils until emulsified.

Tomato and basil

INGREDIENTS

1 large ripe tomato, core cut out, roughly chopped

1 garlic clove, sliced

¼ tsp smoked paprika

2 tbsp cider vinegar

100ml (scant ½ cup) olive oil

1 handful basil leaves

Fresh and light, this is great tossed through blanched beans and feta, drizzled over fish steaks or lamb chops, or spooned over a mozzarella bruschetta and topped with snipped mint. You can make it up to 1 day in advance, but make sure you give it a good shake before using it.

[METHOD]

Put everything in a jug blender and blitz for 30 seconds on high speed. Add salt and coarsely ground black pepper to taste.

Caper, yogurt, argan oil and citrus

INGREDIENTS

150ml (⅔ cup) Greek-style plain yogurt

3 tbsp argan oil (or use extra virgin olive oil)

4 tbsp orange juice

3 tbsp lemon juice

½ tsp orange zest

½ tsp lemon zest

1 tbsp snipped chives

1 tbsp roughly chopped capers

This is more in the style of an American salad cream than a dressing. Spoon it over sliced canteloupe melon and apple salad, or over poached eggs and grilled (broiled) ham on toast with some dill snipped on top. It's also good on poached or steamed fish and poultry. Replace the Greek-style yogurt with plain ewes' milk or goats' milk yogurt for a different flavour. Argan oil adds a delicious richness to this and is well worth using if you have it. Keep in the fridge and use within 2 days.

[METHOD]

Place all the ingredients in a bowl and whisk together. Taste for seasoning; you will probably need to add about ¼ teaspoon of salt.

Coconut, tamarind and star anise

INGREDIENTS

400ml (13½ fl. oz.) can coconut milk (unsweetened)

3 tbsp tamarind paste (more or less to taste)

5cm (2in.) piece ginger, peeled and thinly sliced

½ red chilli, chopped

1 star anise, roughly crushed

½ tsp lime zest, finely grated

4 tbsp lime juice

1 tbsp fish sauce

Three of my favourite ingredients all together! This 'cooked' dressing goes really well tossed through a roast sweet potato (or pumpkin) and bean salad topped with toasted cashews or pumpkin seeds. It's also delicious with thinly sliced grilled (broiled) beef tossed with raw red onions and lots of coriander (cilantro), or spooned over barbecued meat or fish. You can store it in the fridge, but bring it back to room temperature, or warm it slightly, before using, as it'll be quite thick when chilled. It will keep in the fridge for 5 days.

[METHOD]

Place everything except the lime juice and fish sauce in a small pan and slowly bring to the boil. Lower the heat to a rapid simmer and cook until reduced by a third. Add the lime juice and fish sauce and simmer for 5 minutes. Strain and leave to cool.

Opposite page: Coconut, tamarind and star anise (left);
Caper, yogurt, argan oil and citrus (right).

Yogurt, hazelnut, apple and lemon

INGREDIENTS

150ml (⅔ cup) ewes' milk yogurt (or goats' or cows' milk yogurt)

2 tbsp lemon juice

3 tbsp apple juice

2 tsp English or Dijon mustard

2 tbsp hazelnut oil (or walnut oil)

2 tbsp finely chopped roasted hazelnuts

This chunky dressing is good spooned over summer-ripened heritage tomatoes or wedges of iceberg lettuce and slivers of apple, or tossed with chilled cooked rice or pasta, sliced chicken and lots of herbs. The apple juice adds some sweetness, but you can replace it with a different type of fruit juice or a little honey and cold water if you prefer. It will keep in the fridge for 2 days.

[METHOD]

Place everything in a bowl and whisk together. Taste for seasoning.

261

Black vinegar, ginger, sesame and honey

INGREDIENTS

1 tbsp runny honey

2 tsp English mustard

1 tsp finely chopped or grated ginger

4 tbsp black vinegar

1 tsp soy sauce (or ¼ tsp salt)

2 tbsp toasted sesame oil

4 tbsp sunflower oil

Black vinegar is a lovely aged sweet and mildly spiced vinegar from China, easily sourced from a Chinese food shop. It has lovely smoky notes along with, often, hints of orange. You can replace it with a good aged balsamic vinegar instead. Use it to dress sliced tomatoes with mozzarella and basil leaves, to drizzle over any poached chicken or pork salad, or toss it with green and yellow beans and sesame seeds. It will keep in the fridge for 5 days.

[METHOD]

Put the honey, mustard, ginger, black vinegar, soy sauce and 2 tablespoons of cold water in a jar and shake vigorously to dissolve the honey. Add the oils and shake again.

Smoked paprika, garlic and thyme

INGREDIENTS

½ tsp sweet smoked paprika

1 garlic clove, finely crushed

½ tsp thyme leaves

100ml (scant ½ cup) extra virgin olive oil

2½ tbsp red wine vinegar

This Spanish-style dressing is great drizzled over grilled (broiled) prawns (shrimp), or tossed with clams that have been steamed open. It also pairs well with sliced figs that have been sprinkled with grated (shredded) manchego, or spooned over duck-fat roast potatoes. It will keep in the fridge for 3 days.

[METHOD]

Put the paprika, garlic, thyme and 2 tablespoons of the oil in a small pan and place over a medium heat. Cook, stirring continuously, until the garlic has turned golden and is sizzling. Remove from the heat and tip into a heatproof jar or bowl. Gently whisk in the remaining oil, vinegar and ¼ teaspoon of salt and leave to cool.

Opposite, from left to right: Black vinegar, ginger, sesame and honey; Smoked paprika, garlic and thyme; Sherry vinegar and olive.

Sherry vinegar and olive

INGREDIENTS

100ml (scant ½ cup) extra virgin olive oil

1 garlic clove, finely chopped

½ tsp finely chopped fresh herbs (a mix of thyme, oregano and rosemary)

¼ tsp cumin seeds, toasted and crushed

30g (1oz./2½ tbsp) finely chopped pitted olives

2 tbsp sherry vinegar

This chunky dressing is great spooned over roast root vegetables, roast pork, poached chicken or confit duck legs. Any top-quality olives work well here, but green olives will pair better with white meat or fish, and black olives with red meats and roast vegetables. It will keep in the fridge for 2 weeks.

[METHOD]

Place 2 tablespoons of the oil in a small pan and add the garlic, herbs and cumin seeds. Place over a medium—low heat and cook until the garlic is just turning golden, stirring all the time. Tip into a heatproof jar. Pour on the remaining oil and leave for 5 minutes.

Add the olives and sherry vinegar. The olives will be salty so taste the dressing before adding salt.

Shake well before using.

Mayonnaise

INGREDIENTS

1 whole egg

1 egg yolk

2 tsp English mustard

1 tsp cider vinegar (or any white vinegar)

200ml (¾ cup + 2 tsp) sunflower or light olive oil

3½ tbsp virgin rapeseed oil

I thought it necessary to give a recipe for mayonnaise in this book as it's synonymous with salads and you can personalize it by adding all sorts of flavours, from chopped chillies or anchovies to orange zest, shredded herbs or puréed confit garlic. You can either make it in a small food processor or using an electric beater, or simply make it slowly using a hand whisk and bowl. By using a whole egg and a yolk, you're unlikely ever to split your mayonnaise again. I used delicious golden-coloured virgin rapeseed oil to finish my mayonnaise, but you could use extra virgin olive oil. It will keep in the fridge for 3 days.

[METHOD]

Whisk the egg and yolk vigorously with the mustard and vinegar and a little salt. Slowly, drop by drop if whisking by hand, drizzle in the sunflower oil. Once you've added a few tablespoons, you can begin to speed up the drizzling. If you're using a food processor, you can work more quickly. (The reason you need to go slowly is to prevent the mayonnaise from splitting.) Once you have added all the sunflower oil, slowly pour in the rapeseed oil. Taste for seasoning, then add a teaspoon of warm water very quickly at the end, which helps stabilize it.

Condensed milk wasabi 'mayonnaise'

When I was a child growing up in New Zealand, this (apart from the wasabi) was what we called mayonnaise, which is hilarious when I think of what a real mayonnaise is – this contains neither eggs nor oil! The combination of sweet and sour accounted for much of its appeal. I've used wasabi paste in place of the traditional mustard powder here as it goes so well with the sweetness of the condensed milk. Use it to dress coleslaw, mix in chopped gherkins and capers to make a sweet-'n'-spicy tartare sauce, or stir curry powder into it (really!) and toss with chopped boiled eggs, sliced bananas and potatoes for a fabulous quirky potato salad. It will keep in the fridge for up to a week.

INGREDIENTS

1 x 400g (14oz.) can sweetened condensed milk

100ml (scant ½ cup) malt vinegar

2 tbsp wasabi paste (or more, to taste; or use mustard powder or English mustard)

[METHOD]

Whisk everything together briskly with ½ teaspoon of salt for 20 seconds. It will thicken as it sits, so leave it for 20 minutes. If you want to thin it, whisk in some milk.

INGREDIENTS

2 black garlic cloves, sliced

1 garlic clove, sliced

100ml (scant ½ cup) milk

220ml (scant 1 cup) sunflower oil

Egg-free milk aioli

Weird as it seems, this is incredibly simple to make and pretty much foolproof if you have a stick blender (or a jug blender for larger amounts). Aioli, or alioli as the Spanish call it, is a garlic mayonnaise. This egg-free version only has three ingredients apart from seasoning so it can be useful for those with food intolerances – although it does contain milk. I used black garlic in this as I wanted to serve it with the guinea fowl (game hen) on page 218, but you can just as easily make it with plain or smoked garlic. You can also add a few basil, tarragon or young thyme leaves when you first begin blending the garlic and milk. This recipe will probably make more than you need, but it will keep for 4 days in the fridge.

[METHOD]

Using a stick blender, blitz the garlic and milk in a narrow vessel for 15 seconds. Slowly but steadily drizzle in half the oil, then blitz in ½ teaspoon of salt. Continue to blitz in the remaining oil.

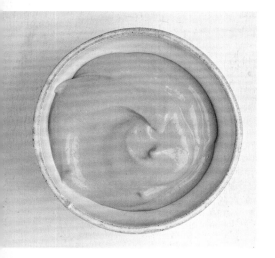

About the author

PETER GORDON was born in the New Zealand coastal town of Whanganui, and collated his first cookbook aged four. After moving to Melbourne in 1981, and completing a four-year cookery apprenticeship, his spirit of adventure and culinary curiosity led him to travel through Asia for a year. This life-changing experience was to become a major influence on his culinary style. In 1986, he moved back to Wellington to become the Head Chef at the original Sugar Club restaurant, a role that established his reputation as a chef. His entrepreneurial spirit combined with his desire to expand his culinary horizons further triggered his move to London in 1989. There he gradually introduced his eclectic style of food, now called fusion, and won wide acclaim for his cooking at the two London branches of The Sugar Club, in Notting Hill and west Soho.

These days, Peter has restaurants in London (The Providores and Tapa Room in Marylebone and Kopapa in Covent Garden) and Auckland (Bellota and The Sugar Club, the fourth iteration of this iconic restaurant brand). He is also a founder of artisan doughnut company Crosstown Doughnuts, which launched in London in April 2014.

This is Peter's eighth cookbook and he has contributed to more than a dozen others. He has appeared on British television, in programmes like Saturday Kitchen and Nigel Slater and Jamie Oliver's Channel 4 food series, as well as being a guest judge on MasterChef in both the UK and New Zealand. Most recently, he presented and was the executive producer of Native Kitchen (TV3 and Māori Television in NZ), a 10-part TV series in which he mentored a group of aspiring young Māori chefs through a 10-day culinary boot camp.

In 1999, Peter was the first to receive the New Zealander of the Year award from The New Zealand Society in London. He is widely recognized as an ardent promoter of the food industry, and in 2009, he was awarded an ONZM (Officer of the New Zealand Order of Merit – the NZ equivalent of an OBE), presented to him by HRH The Queen at Windsor Castle for his services to the food industry.

Index

Acknowledgements

Rather like a salad, this book is a combination of so many different components and people. Thank you to Lorraine Martin for making me 'get it together' in the first place, and to my wonderful agent Heather Holden Brown for sealing the deal! Jacqui Small, Fritha Saunders, Emma Heyworth-Dunn and the JS team, thank you for your ongoing support. Thanks, too, to Caz Hildebrand, Josh and Ashlea from Here Design for combining the images and text in such beautifully creative ways and for Caz's art direction. Photographer Lisa Linder, and right-hand-woman Dom, have turned the ideas in my head and on my chopping board into tasty and gorgeous images, styling as we moved along with Wei Tang's platters, plates and surfaces. Anne McDowall edited and tweaked, queried and quizzed the text into shape. Local London Fields' businesses have been brilliant providores: Fin and Flounder (fish suppliers obviously) and Hill & Szrok (master butcher and cook shop) where I've bought my meat and had numerous dinners post shoots with Alex, Tom and Luca. Stephane and his team at L'eau a la Bouche have sold me gorgeous cheeses, smoked garlic and other foodie treats. Umut is my local Turkish shop selling the most fabulous seasonal vegetables, as does my restaurant supplier 2-Serve with their early morning home drop-offs. My London restaurant teams supported my time working on this project and often helped me cook on the shoots: Lucy, Ben, Polly, Ollie, Paul, Matthew, Young Dave and Jon. And Michael McGrath, Adam Wills, Peter Bezuijen, Rachel Cooper and Lisa Herriett, thanks for all your support!

272